2-19-64

Voices of the Passion

Voices of the Passion

Meditations for the Lenten and Easter Season

by

O. P. Kretzmann and A. C. Oldsen

Augsburg Publishing House · Minneapolis

VOICES OF THE PASSION

Printed and manufactured in the United States of America
by Augsburg Publishing House, Minneapolis 15, Minnesota

Foreword

THE great continuing task of the Christian ministry in every age and every circumstance is the preaching of the Word. To men and women in the mainstream of historic Christianity this is a truism. Strangely enough, however, it is often ignored, either wilfully or regretfully, under the pressure of twentieth century living. The preacher often forgets that the sermon is the climax of his entire life and activity. As a result there is little power in our preaching. We have forgotten how to speak as dying men to dying men. We have failed to remember that in the divine economy the spoken Word is the vehicle of the life and death of the Savior and the means through which the Holy spirit calls and enlightens the souls of men. C574329

It is generally agreed that the twentieth century ministry is complex and bewildering. There can be no doubt that it makes great demands on the conscientious pastor. His tasks are many and varied. The statement, however, that the modern ministry is more complex than the ministry of previous generations is only partially true. It becomes bewildering only when we succumb to the confusion of routine, or when we lose sight of our one great task. When the work of the ministry is stripped down to its bare essentials, there is still only the charge of St. Paul to Timothy: "Preach the Word." If anything in our ministry helps the preaching of the Word, it should be done; if anything gets in the way of the preaching of the Word, it should be eliminated from the life of the Church. Unceasing preaching of the Word is finally the only standard by which the ministry can be measured. We have not been placed into the world to do a thousand different tasks, to build organizations, or to become good fellows. Our task is simple, straight, and magnificent. It is to preach the Word.

The most difficult type of preaching is the faithful Sunday after Sunday appearance of the same pastor in the same pulpit. Our great preachers are not the occasional orators who dust off a brilliant effort, change the introduction, and recite the same sermon eloquently from Coast to Coast. They may draw crowds, but they are not the great preachers of any given generation. On the other hand, the man who preaches to the same people every Sunday, quietly and relentlessly building them into eternity, has the qualities of true greatness. When he ascends his pulpit on Sunday morning he knows all the problems and weaknesses of the individual member of his flock. In the rear seat is John, who is having trouble breaking himself of the drinking habit. To the right is Mary, who is unhappy with an unbelieving husband. Back in the corner is young Bill, who it getting into bad company. To these men and women, close and dear to him, he preaches every Sunday. His task is to bring them a little closer to heaven, to make their eyes a little clearer and their souls a little cleaner. This is far from easy. It is, however, yesterday, today, and tomorrow, a glorious work, and in the final balance of the books of God, a singularly rewarding task.

What is required for this central task of the Christian preacher? First of all, faith! He must believe in the power of his message. He must have faith in the capacity of the reborn soul to come closer to the Yeahs and Amens of God. He must be certain that the individuals to whom he speaks, no matter how weak and wayward, can walk in the way of the Cross and climb the steeps of heaven. His sermon must be a helping and encouraging hand.

Good Sunday after Sunday preaching requires work. No good sermon was ever shaken out of a sleeve. Behind it is always a long period of living with God and His Word. It requires much study and reading of the Bible. It demands a profound and sympathetic insight into the mystery of the human soul. No science or knowledge of man is foreign to a good sermon. A single sermon may be the result of many years of work.

Technically, vast changes have come over our preaching during the past fifty years. The florid, oratorical style of the nineteenth century has given way to a new simplicity and directness. Undoubtedly the radio has had much to do with this change. The twentieth century man and woman is no longer interested in the shouting, arm waving preacher. They want a man to stand up and talk. They want their preacher to be a man in the Way talking to the man in the street.

The readers of this volume will understand that these addresses are not sermons in the usual and accepted sense of the term. The authors are deeply conscious of their shortcomings if they should be measured by sermonic standards. They are rather meditations whose form and content were dictated by the comparative brevity of a Lenten devotion and the cosmopolitan character of audiences consisting of a cross-section of American life, many college students, and a large number of visitors. The seven meditations on the Words from the Cross were prepared for one of the three-hour devotions which many of our pastors have been arranging for Good Friday. It should be noted also that all the meditations were presented in a parish which includes

the members of a university. Such a situation presents unusual difficulties and opportunities. To arrest the attention
of the younger generation, especially of our college youth,
is always a difficult task. The administration of Valparaiso
University is deeply grateful to the Lord of the Church for
the remarkable work of Pastor Oldsen in whom the University has found a man of deep devotion to his work, of
sympathetic understanding of the intellectual and spiritual
problems of youth and of unusual power in the pulpit.

It is our hope and prayer that this little volume will add
a small and humble note of devotion and praise to the holy
name of our blessed Redeemer.

O. P. KRETZMANN

Contents

VOICES OF THE PASSION

MEDITATIONS ON
THE SEVEN WORDS FROM THE CROSS

Meditations on Pontius Pilate and Dismas, and on the Seven Words from the Cross were contributed by O. P. Kretzmann and the balance by A. C. Oldsen.

Voices of the Passion

JUDAS

Judas Iscariot, who also betrayed him.
—MATT. 10:4b.

IF the characters who played a part in the story of our Savior's Passion could speak to us now, out of their unique experience, what would they say? They were part of the only generation privileged to be contemporaries of God's Son in human form, and they were among the few members of that generation who were with Christ when His life on earth came to a close. If they could come back, knowing something of our modern life and thoughts, our hates and loves, our fears and hopes, and tell their story in our language, what would they say to us for a time like this? It can never be. They are gone from the earth these many years. Out of their recorded stories, however, they do still speak to us, clearly and forcefully, if we will but listen. To imagine what they might say, if they could appear in person, is impressive and instructive. If Judas, let us say, were now here, this might be his story:

I, Judas, can tell only of deepest tragedy. I was a man who lived close to heaven, but ended in hell. I was a man who abused the restricted privilege of apostleship and made of the highest opportunity a frightful calamity. Sometimes one or the other of your generation tries to defend me by seeking to demonstrate that everything I did was nobly impelled. It is no use. And it is not true. Not one of the Gospel writers neglects to add to my name the reproachful epithet, "who also betrayed him."[1] One of your greatest preachers says that

---

[1] Matt. 10:4; Mark 3:19; Luke 6:16; John 18:2.

while Christ was God Incarnate, I was the devil incarnate. I still am the target of some of the most vehement and heartless denunciations hurled from your Christian pulpits. The worst of you throw stones at me.

Listen to my story as I plead, not for forgiveness, but for understanding. Forget for a moment, if you can, the dark and terrible close of my life, and remember that I was human. I acted like a human being. What I did any human is capable of doing, even you! When I was born at Kerioth centuries ago, with the taint of original sin on my baby soul, but not with the actual sin of betrayal, my parents loved me dearly and thanked the God of Israel devoutly for the precious gift. I know, because they picked for me the finest of names. They called me Judas and Judas means "Praise of God." It would have broken their hearts as they bent admiringly over me, to have known that one day Christ would speak of me and say, "It had been better for that man if he had not been born."[2] Little did anyone in our community realize that I alone of all who lived in Kerioth would be remembered in history; less did they imagine that I would go down as the most despicable character of all time.

I was reared like other boys in Judea, taught to know and to believe in the God of our fathers. As I grew to adulthood I developed a deep interest in spiritual matters. Then came the greatest day of my life. The prophet of Nazareth invited me: "Follow me!" It set me on the path that leads to the heights. That puzzles you. You cannot understand why Christ chose a man like me as an Apostle. Forgive me! why did He choose you as a follower? God does not look at what a man

---

[2] Matt. 26:24.

is, but at what, by grace, he may become. Christ saw that I had glorious possibilities. With the best and happiest of intentions I forsook all and followed Him. For about two years I lived with Him: I heard His matchless sermons: I witnessed His divine miracles. But when they killed Him and He left earth for heaven, I killed myself and went to hell.

Let me tell you how it happened. Listen and you will know how a single passion can kill a man's soul, not quickly as a boa constrictor coils itself about a deer and crushes it to death, but gradually and almost imperceptibly as a vine grows round an oak and chokes it. My fall was not a chance happening of an evening; it was a creeping development.

My master passion was greed and, since I was treasurer for our small group, temptation visited me often and long. We had little in our coffers, but one day some of it stuck to my fingers and fell into my pocket. As you count sin in your world it was only a little sin. I did not bother to call it sin. Some day I would pay it back, I quietly told myself; and if I did not, the insignificant amount I had taken would not begin to compensate for all the bother I had with the care of the treasury. When you want to sin, the devil is ready to suggest an excuse with which to conceal your baseness even from yourself. As I look back now, I wish I had been caught the first time I stole. If I had, my story might have been written on a higher level. When you get caught at a sin, thank God for it. The sins you get away with harden you and curse you doubly, today and tomorrow. They are the sins you try again.

As time went on I stole more often and larger amounts and with less compunction. My story demonstrates a truth that is as important for your day as it ever was: life is lived on an incline on which it is easier to fall than it is to rise.

Think not I was not warned. Now the admonitions of
Christ sound clear and strong to me like a fog horn in the
stillness of the night. There was the time He was speaking to
us disciples and to the multitude, "Beware of the leaven of the
Pharisees, which is hypocrisy. For there is nothing covered
that shall not be revealed; neither hid, that shall not be known.
. . . Take heed, and beware of covetousness: for a man's life
consisteth not in the abundance of the things which he posses-
seth."[3] His warnings were like tracer bullets aimed at me and
leaving a trail I felt all could see. Never say God does not
warn you in your sin. You ignore His admonition until the day
after the fall, and then you look back and wail, "How could
I have been so blind and deaf!"

My story shows also that sin grows like a cancer. It may
begin with a single passion, but gradually it contaminates
other emotions and develops them abnormally. The joy I at
first experienced in the companionship of the Apostles gave
way to fear that they would eventually discover my dis-
honesty. The love I had for Christ, when I began to follow
Him, turned to bitter hatred as His perfection became an
ever-present and provoking rebuke. Withal I realized that He
who knew the thoughts of a Samaritan woman, could read
the secrets in the heart of a Judas. Bit by bit dissolved the
sincerity in which I had joined the company of Christ, until
I became a consummate hypocrite.

I remember the meal in the home of Simon the leper. Mary
of the loving heart anointed Christ with precious ointment. I
objected most vehemently to the waste and suggested that the
ointment should have been sold and the money given to the

---

[3] Luke 12:1, 2, 15.

poor. My thought was that I could have done the distributing, some of it to myself. When Christ lauded Mary for her devotion, it was too much. I went to the priests and made a damnable covenant to sell Him into death for one-third the amount Mary had spent for the ointment.

In one of His sermons Christ took an imaginary scale. On one arm He piled all the wealth of the world, its gold and jewels, its mountains and lakes, its factories and homes. On the other arm He laid a single soul. The scale moved. The soul was of greater value. "What shall it profit a man, if he shall gain the whole world, and lose his own soul?"[4] I took a scale too. On one arm I placed the divine Lord, my soul and its eternal destiny. On the other arm I put thirty pieces of silver, less than twenty dollars in your money, the price of the meanest slave. My perverted scale moved—in the other direction. I thought the money had greater value.

I remember the meal in the upper room. I was there with the black plans I carried in my heart. Nothing so corrupts a heart as the plan for a sin. Christ was still warning me: "One of you which eateth with me shall betray me."[5] I had to play my hypocritical part to the end; with the puzzled Apostles I therefore asked, "Lord, is it I?"[6] He was still loving and considerate. Instead of pointing at me and saying in righteous anger "Yes!", He replied softly and enigmatically, "He it is, to whom I shall give a sop, when I have dipped it."[7] He dipped it and gave it to me.

Now my story, as you know it, runs quickly to its terrible

---

[4] Mark 8:36.
[5] Mark 14:18.
[6] Matt. 26:22.
[7] John 13:26.

end. It comes back to me like a terrifying dream. I had led the
mob to the garden and was about to betray Christ with the
usual greeting of a kiss. Hard man that I was, it was not
easy. As I looked into His face I half expected Him to damn
me with all the vehemence of His divine indignation. But all
I saw in that face was love and pain. "Friend," He said.
Think of it; He still called me friend! "Friend, wherefore
art thou come?"[8] He knew, but He wanted me to put the
betrayal into words and to see how diabolic was my sin.
Instead, I kissed Him.

With that, my world crashed! A horror swept over me,
which, pray God, you may never know. The enormity of my
guilt overwhelmed me. Sin looks so different after it has
been committed! In temptation sin is appealing, like red wine
sparkling in a glass; in the accomplished act sin stings like
an adder.[9]

Scarcely knowing what I did, I sat down by myself that
dark night and looked out of the window of the past. The
scenes of my association with Christ, especially of the last
hours, tumbled through my mind in a tumult of confusion.
It began happily, "Follow me!" but ended tragically, "Judas,
betrayest thou the Son of man with a kiss?"[10] Christ's sermon
in the majestic beauty of the mountain, "Where your
treasure is, there will your heart be also. . . No man can serve
two masters: for either he will hate the one, and love the
other; or else he will hold to one, and despise the other,"[11]
and in my pocket, the silver coins with the ironic superscrip-

---

[8] Matt. 26 :50.
[9] Prov. 23 :31-32.
[10] Luke 22 :48.
[11] Matt. 6 :21, 24.

tion, "Jerusalem, the Holy"—the warning of Christ, "One of you shall betray me,"[12] and the smile of Caiaphas when I asked, "What will you give me?"[13]—the song of the children on Sunday, "Hosanna," and the foul threats of an unprincipled mob—Christ washing our feet and my tasting of the sop.

Two years before I had met Him, loved him, and followed Him. Blessed thought! I began to drift and to hate Him. Cursed thought! Matthew, Mark, and Luke tell how bitterly Peter wept that same night. Do you think I did not cry? Where I sat that night the sands were wet with my hot tears.

For a moment I turned and looked out of the window of the future. It was black as midnight, with no glimmer of hope.

The money jingled uneasily in my pocket. It suggested a last desperate action. I went to those with whom I had conspired, "I have sinned," I pleaded, "in that I have betrayed the innocent blood."[14] Daily they offered temple sacrifices for the penitent, and millions had received from them the assurance of sins forgiven. But not I. They only took my burning heart and dipped it into their cold and scornful indifference. "What is that to us?" they said with a smirk; "See thou to that."[15] That was too much. I took the money in my trembling hands and hurled it into the temple. But this act of madness did not relieve me. Sin is marked on the soul and you cannot throw it away with your hands.

---

[12] Matt. 26:21.
[13] Matt. 26:15.
[14] Matt. 27:4.
[15] Matt. 27:4.

You cannot touch the sin that has been committed, not even with penitence and tears. Only God can take it away.

Never go to the world with your confession of sin. It has no concern for sin and no interest in confession. It will only be amused. Rather go to Him who invites, "Come unto Me, all ye that labor and are heavy laden, and I will give you rest."[16] It is my tragedy that I did not go.

For a fatal moment I stood at the last great crossroads. To the right was Jerusalem and the loving Christ. Peter went there and found the peace of forgiveness. I did not find it, not because God refused me, but because I did not ask for it. I took the road to the left. It led to a tree in the valley, death by my own hand, the condemnation of all generations, and hell without end.

Before I leave, allow me one word more. I was not the last suicide. Not only Japanese take their own life. On an average day more than sixty die in your country by their own hand. They are among the world's most misunderstood people. My heart goes out to them.

In an audience of this size there will be some who know the torment of suicidal impulses and others who will yet discover their horror. Suicides fall into three general classes. There are those whose minds are deranged and who are no more responsible before God or man for their actions than a musician is responsible for the music he is forced to play on a violin with loose and broken strings.

The largest class is made up of those who are afraid of tomorrow, the men usually for economic reasons, the women more often for personal and domestic reasons. The

---
[16] Matt. 11:28.

best advice I can give them, is that they do what I neglected to do. Let them tell their trouble to God and let them discuss their problem with a strong Christian friend or pastor to be assured of God's loving providence also for tomorrow.

The third class is ashamed of yesterday. That was my trouble. I could think only of my sin. You can never think too harshly of your sin; but when you think of it alone, it will drive you to despair. You remember the story of the Prodigal Son.[17] As the wretch sat among the swine, he thought not only of his plight; he thought of the love of his father. "I will arise and go to my father, and will say unto him, 'Father, I have sinned against heaven, and before thee.'" You who are driven to despair over your sin, go home. Go to your heavenly Father and say, "I have sinned. Forgive me for Jesus' sake." And you will sing again. I, Judas, will never sing again.

You probably expect me to say, "Try to forget me!" Instead I say, "Remember me, Judas, 'Praise of God,' who also betrayed Christ." My life will never be an inspiration to you, but it must always be a powerful warning.

---

[17] Luke 15:11-24.

PETER

*Thou shalt be called Cephas, which is by
interpretation, A stone.*—JOHN 1:42b.

NEXT to Christ, which of the characters that walk
through the pages of Bible History would you most
like to have known personally? The answers will vary
widely, but the choice will fall most frequently on Peter.
He was such an intensely human man that we readily see
in him a bit of ourselves. He was a man we would have
learned to know in a short time, and a man we would have
remembered. Of all the Apostles he would have been most
easily recognized. More than likely he would have been the
first to speak to us, the first to offend and the first to
apologize.

Even among the Apostles Peter stands out. Whenever
the Apostles are enumerated in the Bible Peter's name heads
the list.[1] With James and John he was in the Lord's intimate, inner circle of disciples; and in each of the seven
Gospel references to the three, Peter is mentioned first.

In the story of our Savior's suffering and death Peter
moves quickly from one extreme to the other. In doing so,
he is true to his impetuous disposition. Throughout his
life, until his fall, Peter is a child of impulse. One moment
he walks confidently upon the water; three seconds later he
is sinking and calling for help. One minute he makes a
remarkable confession of Christ, "Thou art the Christ, the
Son of the living God" and wins Christ's commendation,
"Blessed art thou, Simon Barjona"; the next minute he pro-

---

[1] Matt. 10:2; Mark 3:16; Luke 6:14; Acts 1:13.

tests against Christ's announcement of His impending Passion, "Be it far from Thee, Lord!" and merits Christ's rebuke, "Get thee behind me, Satan."[2]   On the way to the garden he vows his readiness to die for his Lord; in the garden he cannot keep awake for his Lord.   When the mob comes to take Christ, he draws his unfamiliar sword and shows he has the courage, if need be, to fight the Roman army; when he is in the courtyard, that same evening, among the same enemies, he wilts under the glance of a slave maiden and cowardly denies his Lord.

Yet with all his faults, Peter is a lovable man. The best of us will find inspiration in his life and the worst of us will gain comfort from it. His zeal and impetuosity, the very traits of disposition which led to his downfall, were sanctified by grace and became essential elements of Peter, the Rock. Peter, the man who knew life and sin and Christ, might tell us this story:

I, Peter, was born on the north shore of the beautiful Sea of Galilee. My father John was a fisherman and it was among fishermen that I grew up.   They were men with rough hands and crude manners, but soft hearts; men often deeply religious and yet at times most profane and vulgar. It was on the sea, usually calm and mirror-like, yet sometimes churned without warning by a dreadful tempest, that I spent much of my early years.

When I was a boy, a strange story was told by a group of shepherds, down Bethlehem way. They were frightened in the night by a heavenly glory, they said, and a reassuring angel directed them to a newborn child lying in a manger.

[2] Matt. 16:16-23.

What made it all the more impressive was the announcement of the angel that the child was the long-promised
Christ. Then we heard no more about it, but I often wondered whether I would live to see the Messiah for whom my
people had been waiting many centuries.

I was a man about forty, carrying on my fishing trade
at Bethsaida, when we heard of an extraordinary crusader
who was preaching and baptizing in the wilderness adjoin-
ing the River Jordan. He spoke plainly and earnestly with
an eloquence that was arresting. He spoke directly from
the shoulder, directly to the heart. He was sternly warning
everyone to repent because the long-expected Messiah was
soon to appear. Everywhere he and his soul-searching message were the subject of conversation. People from all over
the land flocked to him. We went too, my brother Andrew
and I, and so profoundly were we impressed that we became his disciples. More eagerly than ever we awaited the
coming of the Savior.

One memorable day Andrew came home with an elec-
trifying announcement. "We have found the Messiah,"[3] he
exclaimed, greatly excited. You will never know what that
meant to us. During the Advent Season some of you try
to put yourself into the expectant frame of mind that was
ours as we waited for the coming of Christ. You can
never do it successfully. You know exactly when you will
observe the anniversary of the Savior's birth. Your choirs
rehearse for the gladsome festival and you have programs
printed in advance. We did not know when Christ was coming. We looked for Him from day to day.

I followed Andrew eagerly as he led me to a man of

---

[3] John 1 :41.

about thirty and indicated that this was the Messiah. As the young man looked at me, He seemed to read my inmost thoughts. I became distressingly aware of much that he saw. He startled me by saying, "Thou art Simon the son of Jona: thou shalt be called Cephas."⁴ He knew my name without an introduction. He gave me a new name, Peter, which means rock. At the time my character was far from being rock-like and He must have known it would take long for me to petrify enough to deserve the name.

For a time several others and I followed Jesus. We attended a wedding at Cana where He amazed us by turning water into wine. We visited Jerusalem where He enraged the religious leaders by driving the traders and money changers from the temple. We stopped at Sychar for two days and when we left, the people of Sychar made Him happy with the confession, "We know that this is indeed the Christ, the Savior of the world."⁵ When we returned to Galilee, we went back to our fishing trade.

We were fishing on the sea one spring day about a year after I had met Christ, when He passed along the shore unexpectedly and called to us, "Come ye after me, and I will make you to become fishers of men."⁶ The next sentence in the Sacred Record thrills me to this day. "And straightway they forsook their nets, and followed him." That was the great turning point in my life and, by the grace of God, I turned in the right direction. How different my life would have been if I had stayed with my nets. I denied Christ later—I cannot forget that; but when

⁴ John 1:42.
⁵ John 4:42.
⁶ Mark 1:17.

He invited me, I accepted. When He gave me work to do,
I did it. When He said "Follow Me!" I followed. You
who criticize me harshly, when He gives you an assignment
(possibly an unpleasant one), do you always carry it out?

I vividly remember many events of my life with Christ.
Let me tell you briefly of two of them. One day He took
James, John, and me into a room in which there was a
dead girl. The professional mourners grinned sardonically
when He told them the girl was merely sleeping. You should
have seen the astounded look on their faces when the girl
walked out a few minutes later. Christ had taken her by
the hand and had called her back to life with an almighty, "I
say unto thee, arise!"[7] I wish you could have been there.
When you lay into their last earthly resting place your beloved dead who have died in the Lord and after the tidal
wave of grief has overwhelmed you, I hope that you can
hear the word of the Savior above the sob and sighing, like
a bell in the storm, "I say unto thee, arise!"

About a year later He took the three of us up the
rough slope of a mountain to a resting place far above
the quiet valley. We were asleep almost as soon as we re-
clined on the grass. Strange things happened while we were
slumbering. We awoke with a start. The face of Christ
was shining like the sun and His clothing was dazzling white.
Moses was there and Elijah. All too quickly a cloud covered the scene of unimaginable glory. The voice of God
spoke from the cloud, "This is my beloved Son: hear Him."[8]
Often I thought of what God said, especially on Good Friday
as I stood at a distance and beheld the cross with moistened

7 Mark 5:41.
8 Mark 9:7.

eyes. I hope that you can hear it when doubts sometimes assail you and you long desperately for truth; namely, "This is my beloved Son: Hear Him."

You are expecting me to say something about my great sin the night of the Savior's trial. May I first tell you how I came to fall? You say it is a wise man who knows his own strength. The man who knows his own weakness is wiser. Knowing one's strength may lead to great accomplishment; knowing one's weakness may prevent great tragedy. I did not know my own weakness.

My greatest weakness was an exaggerated self-confidence. I was too sure of myself. My false pride was in evidence practically every day that I spent in the company of Christ and the Apostles. It is written on many pages of the Gospels. Take, for example, the night we were walking out to Gethsemane. The hour was late and ominous. We walked in darkness and silence until Jesus told us we would desert Him that night.[9] Of course, we all denied it; but I had to stand out in my denial. I did not trust the others, not even my brother Andrew and my good friends James and John. But in one man I had absolute confidence. That man was myself, Peter. I would stand in any storm. I would stay with my Lord when to do so meant death. Think not it was a lightly-given promise. I meant it. I can still remember it; and how I regret it! I was thinking of it when I wrote some thirty-five years later, "Be clothed with humility: for God resisteth the proud, and giveth grace to the humble."[10]

You of the twentieth century put a premium on self-

[9] Matt. 26:31 A.T.
[10] I Peter 5:5.

confidence. You laud the man who is able to stand alone in any situation, the man who asks favors of no one. Books on self-improvement recommend that you "believe in yourself." That is all well and good, if you believe that you are nothing by yourself, but altogether dependent on God. The Bible encourages such confidence. Paul unblushingly boasted, "I can do all things," but he quickly added, "through Christ which strengtheneth me."[11] On another occasion he wrote, "Not that we are sufficient of ourselves to think anything as of ourselves; but our sufficiency is of God."[12]

The Bible cautions repeatedly against pride and a confidence in self alone. Solomon declares, "Pride goeth before destruction, and an haughty spirit before a fall."[13] Again he says, "Seeth thou a man wise in his own conceit? There is more hope of a fool than of him."[14] Paul warns, "Let him that thinketh he standeth take heed lest he fall."[15]

No one knows himself so well that he can be sure of his behavior in an emergency. You have all done things which you once said you would never do. If I could tell you the sins some of you will commit before you leave this life, you would sincerely denounce me. Your athletic directors sometimes give this axiom to their teams: "Concede every opponent the possibility of defeating you, but be determined it will not be this time." The same may be a good axiom for the Christian life: I concede that I am weak enough to fall a victim to any temptation, but I am determined, by the grace of God, it will not happen this time.

---

[11] Phil. 4:13.
[12] II Cor. 3:5.
[13] Prov. 16:18.
[14] Prov. 26:12.
[15] I Cor. 10:12.

I was sure I could not fall. You know what happened. Christ even gave me the details of my fall in advance. Still I boasted it could not happen. But it did!

My swaggering nature took me into the courtyard of the high priest's palace. I joined my enemies around a coal fire, where a question caught me off balance. "Art not thou also one of this man's disciples?"[16] Because I had always acted on the impulse of the moment, this question frightened me into a quick denial. It seemed to be a wise way of avoiding needless danger. I did not know that when you kill truth suddenly and without following a premeditated plan, you soon have to commit deliberate murder.

The temptation came back. This time it was not a question, but a statement of fact addressed not to me, but to those standing around me: "This fellow was also with Jesus of Nazareth."[17] Merely to lie about it again would have been useless. I denied it with an oath! Even that did not convince them.

A third time I was charged with being a follower of Christ, and this time the accusation was supported by evidence. My Galilean brogue betrayed me. I vehemently denied it all with the horrid oaths and curses I had once learned out on the sea. In two years I had not forgotten them. Old habits of sin have a distressing way of coming back to life suddenly and unexpectedly. Not only must you bury them; you must stand guard at the grave for the rest of your life.

I will always be remembered for my shameless denial.

---

[16] John 18:17.
[17] Matt. 26:71.

You have never denied Him, at least not by saying with your lips, "I do not know Christ." But how eloquently you can deny Him with your life! Do men know from your manner of living that you are a sincere follower of Christ, or do they look at your life and never suspect that you are Christian?

If you have denied Him, then stand where I stood that night. Christ passed by and looked at me. What was in that look I will never be able to tell you exactly. It was not a look of rebuke, as some of you insist. There was love in it and understanding. It said to me, "I feel sorry for you, Peter. You failed Me, but I forgive you."

That look opened the gates of my heart to let a flood of tears rush out. I am not ashamed of the way I cried. The world knows of my sin: the world must know also of my remorse. It was a most grievous experience. My cheeks had often been wet with the spray of the sea, but not with tears. When I saw my Savior and recognized my sin—strong man that I was, I had to cry.

You of the twentieth century weep so little over sin. You cry at the movies or while you read a touching story or over the consequences of sin; but how many of you have shed tears over your sin? Your remorse is mild and moderate. Your hearts are so dry, they never want to relieve themselves by tears. I am not encouraging you to affect religious feeling. God does not want it. But God does want you to recognize the damnable difference between what He in His mercy wants you to be, and what you actually are. When you understand that clearly, your eyes too will be moist.

Christ wept as He looked out over Jerusalem and saw the iniquity and spiritual indifference of that unholy place.

If He would look over our world today as He looked over Jerusalem, what would He do? Joseph Hoy has put his answer into a drawing. Over an immense globe that represents our world lies the thorn-crowned figure of Christ, folded hands outstretched, head buried in His arms, weeping. Another has put his answer into verse:

> Over a world
> Bristling with hate, with violence rife,
> Terrified, crazed with murderous strife,
> For greed and conquest spending its life—
> Over a world
> Stricken by war,
> Jesus, our Savior, weeps!
>
> Over a world
> Starving and weary, lost in the night,
> With countless millions in fear and in flight,
> Seeking for refuge and praying for light—
> Over a world
> Stricken with grief,
> Jesus, our Savior, weeps!
>
> Over a world
> Spent with the struggle, asking release,
> Praying that conquest and warfare may cease,
> Weary of conflict and craving for peace—
> Over a world
> Sinful and sad
> Jesus, our Savior, weeps.

I cried over my sin, but there came a time when I dried my tears. Clement tells that for the remainder of my life I fell on my knees whenever I heard a rooster crow, and with bitter weeping asked God for forgiveness. It is not true. According to one tradition my cheeks were marked with furrows down which the tears continued to flow. That is not true either.

My risen Lord appeared to me on Sunday. The Bible is silent about what happened when I was alone with Him whom I had offended so shamelessly.[18] Believe me, He assured me that my sins were forgiven. Thereupon I dried my tears.

Remember me, Peter, not as the man who was afraid of a maiden and who denied Christ with a blasphemous, "I do not even know the man," but instead as the man who gazed calmly at a martyr's death and said confidently. "We cannot but speak the things which we have seen and heard."[19]

---

[18] Luke 24:34.
[19] Acts 4:20.

JOHN

Beloved, if God so loved us, we ought also to love one another.—I JOHN 4:11.

THE story of the Passion tells of the height of God's love and of the depth of man's depravity. It places them side by side and the contrast is terrifying. What makes the story all the more tragic is the fact that practically every character in it, save only our Lord, demonstrates how terrible are the thoughts that proceed out of the heart of man and become the pattern of his behavior. Clearly in evidence are unbelief and intrigue, avarice and theft, disloyalty and betrayal, boasting and denial, overconfidence and cowardice, falsehood and slander, hatred and brutality, fear and murder. Then, like a breath of fresh air in a stuffy room comes the chapter on the loving and faithful John! He does not play his part blamelessly; he does, however, play it more nobly than the others. In paintings of Christ and the Apostles John looks like his Lord. That is not a coincidence.

Before John tells his story, let us make sure we do not misunderstand him. Tender he is, in the full sense of the word, but he is not effeminate. A dreamer he is, in the good sense of the word, but not a man whose feet have never touched the earth. Take a good look at his face, if you get a chance; observe his hands; and notice his muscles. They are rugged and rough and hard. Much of John's life was spent on the sea, rowing in the sun and in the storm, and tugging at the nets. Sometimes John is pictured with a dove; his true symbol is the eagle. This might be his story:

I, John, have a little sermon to preach to you of the

twentieth century. Before I do so, let me tell you about myself. You will then be better able to understand my sermon.

I was born on the shore of the sea made famous by Christ. My first home was at Bethsaida, just east of where the Jordan rushed into the Sea of Galilee. The time was the very age I would have chosen, had the choice been made. I was a contemporary of Jesus of Nazareth, John the Baptist, and Paul of Tarsus. I became personally and intimately acquainted with all of them. My father's name was Zebedee and my mother's Salome. Your scholars have been much concerned about my mother's probable relationship to Mary, the mother of Christ. Some of them insist that Mary and Salome were sisters and that Christ and I were therefore cousins. What difference does it make? My blood relationship to Christ is unimportant; my heart's relationship to Him is all-important!

From an early age my parents instructed me in the religion of the Old Testament. They did not wait for the Church to teach their child about God, as some of you do. We had a proverb in our day which said, "Only the vilest of men does not teach his child religion." Yours is a vile age, is it not?

My father was a master fisherman and taught my older brother James and me the way of the fish and the way of the sea. I was well trained to fish with hook and line and with various kinds of nets. Fishing was to become my life's occupation.

At thirteen I walked almost a hundred miles to Jerusalem and to the temple—I can still feel a bit of the thrill of it—

and became a "Son of the Law," a full member of the Church.

Often while I was out on the sea in the stillness of the night, with the bright stars twinkling above me and their reflections dancing on the water all around me, or while I was sitting on the white sandy shore in the warm morning sun, untangling nets and removing the weeds, questions came to me as they must sometimes come to you. What does life mean? A short, sad song and then silence forever? Was there a time when the sea and the stars did not exist? Where did they and I come from? What will eventually happen to us?

One day I met a man who impressed me profoundly. He began to convince me that the answers my parents had given to my questions were correct. You know him as John the Baptist. In all your world no man is like him. His character was like granite and when he thundered at you, "Repent ye!" it was as though the book of your life had fallen open before God. We loved the man and we became his disciples. Yet always we feared him and the more we heard him preach in his rough, camel-hair mantle, the more we felt the need for something to cover the ugly sins of our life.

We were listening to John one time when messengers of the Pharisees came and asked if he was the promised Messiah. He answered emphatically, "I am not the Christ!" He added, "There standeth one among you, whom ye know not; he it is, who coming after me is preferred before me, whose shoe's latchet I am not worthy to unloose."[1] You could feel that no one understood exactly what he meant. The next day John suddenly pointed to a man who was passing near

---

[1] John 1:20, 26, 27.

and said (as though it was the greatest moment in his life), "Behold the Lamb of God, which taketh away the sin of the world. This is he of whom I said, After me cometh a man which is preferred before me: for he was before me. And I knew him not: but that he should be made manifest to Israel, therefore am I come baptizing with water."[2]

He was pointing to Christ, the Prophet of Nazareth, son of a gracious woman named Mary, and, as we thought, of her husband Joseph. It all made a soul-stirring impression on us. Andrew and I followed the retreating figure of Christ. He waited for us and then asked kindly, "What seek ye?"[3] Hesitantly we responded with another question, "Master, where dwellest thou?"[4] He invited us to come along.

We spent several hours with Him that afternoon and evening and when we went to bed that night we felt in our inmost hearts that the long-cherished hope of our fathers had been fulfilled. This was truly the Christ, the Messiah!

How happy I was when He later came to me, as I was mending nets, and asked me to follow Him! He meant far more to me than my business. I therefore left everything and followed Him. For two years I lived at His side. I was with Him in the storm on the sea, in the glory of the morning on the mountain, in the devotional quiet of the temple. Wherever He went, mutitudes crowded about Him. When you go to Church today, you usually fill the back pews first until gradually you are forced to sit near the front. It was different in Christ's day. He could not keep the

---

[2] John 1 :29-31.
[3] John 1 :38.
[4] John 1 :38.

listeners back far enough. He even got into a boat once and taught the people from the sea, where they could not crowd about Him. When He preached, you could not help listening. The scribes and Pharisees were always quoting the authorities. He did not have to quote; he could introduce His thoughts with, "I say unto you."

I wish I could tell you everything that happened during the short years we were together. There is not time. I did write five of the books in the New Testament. Have you read them?

There came a day when Christ frightened us by saying that He would have to go to Jerusalem to suffer and die.[5] We could not believe it. All too soon, less than a year later, His prophecy was going into heart-rending fulfillment. Almost in a daze I was shuffling to a little hill outside the walls of Jerusalem. Late the night before I had lain at the bosom of the Lord I loved so dearly. Blessed memory! Now they had nailed Him to a cross on that little hill. I could not keep away. I had to look into His face once more. Once more I had to hear a word from Him. The women were sobbing softly when I joined them at the foot of the cross. It was so different from what we had expected. We could not speak. It was not necessary. He understood. At last He raised His head and looked first at Mary, His mother, and then at me. To her He said gently, "Woman, behold thy son!" And then to me, "Behold thy mother!"[6] I could still hear the words clearly when I wrote them into my Gospel more than fifty years later. I can hear them even now.

---

[5] Matt. 16:21.
[6] John 19:26, 27.

We were almost desperate with grief when Joseph and Nicodemus buried Him in a garden late that afternoon. I can talk about it now without tears. He rose again on Sunday morning. I saw Him again, not in shame but in glory. I saw Him rise majestically to His home in heaven.

I wish you could have stood with me at the foot of the cross, if only for a moment. There would have swept over you, as it swept over me and over the malefactor and over the centurion, a glorious realization of the boundless love of God for the world of sinful men and therefore also for you. You may think me a bit egotistical for referring to myself in the Gospel with the epithet "the disciple whom Jesus loved." That is not egotism. That is the foundation of true Christian Faith. There can be no faith without it. He loves you, too, no matter who you are and no matter what you have done. Here is a thought to give you comfort. Has the world forsaken you? God loves you. Is your future uncertain? God loves you. Do you understand how severely you have offended God? He still loves you. Write behind your name what I wrote and see what it does for you. John Smith, the man Jesus loves. Mary Jones, the woman Jesus loves. Jackie Brown, the child Jesus loves.

When you begin to see the great love God has for you, your emotions will respond in "an interlocking chain." If God loves you infinitely, and demonstrated his love for you so preëminently, how can you help loving God? "We love him because He first loved us."[7]

In your sermons about me you sometimes stress my loyalty. You speak of my courage that took me into the courtyard among my Lord's aroused enemies. You refer

---

[7] I John 4:19.

to my zeal and devotion in telling others of the Savior, which put me into prison and carried me in my old age a lonely exile to the Island of Patmos. My loyalty and courage and devotion do not stand alone. They are results. They flowed from my love for Christ. You can be that loyal, that fearless, that devoted, if you will love Him as I did. It was my love for Christ that took me into the courtyard and to the foot of the cross. It was my love for Christ that moved me into a dangerous mission field. It was my love for Christ that enabled me to stand on trial and, together with Peter, in the face of dire threats, refuse to cease preaching and confessing.[8] Because "there is no fear in love,"[9] we were not afraid.

When you have stood at the foot of the cross and when the love God has for you, has overwhelmed you quite, you will be ready for the line I wrote in my first epistle, "Beloved, if God so loved us, we ought also to love one another."[10] I wish you could see clearly what your world looks like with its ugly scars of many a war, and especially with the new wound, deep and painful, that your generation has been inflicting.

The Persians were telling a legend in my day that sets forth in striking manner the difference between what the world of men is and what God wants it to be. This was the legend: A man finds himself in a great banquet hall, brilliantly lighted and splendidly decorated. Many guests are seated at tables laden with a sumptuous and tempting meal. But no one is eating. You see, somebody has tied a stick

---

[8] Acts 4 :20.
[9] I John 4 :18.
[10] I John 4 :11.

to every arm so that no one can bend an elbow. The result is that while everyone can touch the food, no one can bring it to his mouth. In exasperation the guests have begun to quarrel and to hit and kill one another. The man leaves the hall, deeply distressed by what he has seen.

He finds himself suddenly in another banquet hall, as brilliantly lighted and as splendidly decorated as the first. There are as many guests and the food is the same. Again the arms of each guest have been tied in such a manner that everyone can touch the food, but no one can bring it to his lips. Yet all are eating, happily and merrily. There is no strife. They have learned that while no one can feed himself, they can all feed one another.

There you have the difference between the world of men as it is, and the world of men as it might be and as God wants it to be. The world of men as it is: a vast hall; decorated as only God can decorate; supplied with food and resources as only God can supply; guests numbering over two billion and able to live—if they will but love God and one another—happily and at peace. Instead they are hitting and killing one another, because most of them are concerned chiefly with what each can get for himself.

Do you have any conception of the evil your generation has wrought on the face of the earth? Some of your experts have estimated, conservatively at that, that the total cost of World War II, including the property destroyed, will be in excess of one trillion dollars. Think of what love for the fellow man could have done with that money. It could have built for each of the 400,000 groups of 5,000 people throughout the world, including the masses of India, China, and Japan, a school for $275,000, a church for

$150,000, a hospital for $100,000, a home for the destitute for $50,000, a library for $50,000, and a park for $25,000. If the amount of money left after all these had been built were then put into an endowment fund, the annual interest on the fund would perpetually pay the salaries of 20 teachers, 10 nurses, two doctors, two clergymen, two librarians, and two superintendents for the park and home.

And there are still some who ridicule Christ and call Him an idle dreamer because He preached, "Love one another, as I have loved you."[11] Will men ever heed?

I lived to an old age and survived the other Apostles. Among my pupils were Polycarp, Papias, and Ignatius. Irenaeus, disciple of Polycarp, tells that I spent my closing years at Ephesus and died in the reign of Trajan, the Roman Emperor from 98 to 117.

Best-known among the stories of my closing years is that about my last, short sermon. When I was too old and feeble to walk to church, loving arms carried me to the service and supported me while I sincerely and tenderly preached my brief sermon. It was always the same, "Little children, love one another." It is my message to you. Eastwood has put the story into poetry. On my return to Ephesus I speak:

What say you, friends?

That this is Ephesus, and Christ has gone
Back to His kingdom? Ay, 'tis so, 'tis so;
I know it all; and yet, just now I seemed
To stand once more upon my native hills
And touch my Master....

---

[11] John 13:34.

Up! Bear me to my church once more,
There let me tell them of a Savior's love;
For by the sweetness of my Master's voice
I think He must be very near....

They carry me to the church and I continue:

So raise up my head;

How dark it is! I cannot seem to see
The faces of my flock. Is that the sea
That murmurs so, or is it weeping? Hush!
My little children! God so loved the world
He gave His Son; so love ye one another,
Love God and men.

CAIAPHAS

*Caiaphas was he, which gave counsel to the Jews
that it was expedient that one man should die
for the people.—JOHN 18:14.*

WHO is primarily responsible for the crucifixion of
Christ? Not Pilate, for when Christ was brought to
him on Friday morning the sentence had been pronounced,
"He is guilty of death,"[1] and Christ Himself said to Pilate,
"He that delivered me unto thee hath the greater sin."[2] Not
Judas, for when he asked the priests, "What will you give
me, and I will deliver him unto you?"[3] the plans for the
execution had long been made. Not the mob, for it had
sung "Hosanna" in sincere joy on Sunday and was echoing
the desires of only a few leaders when it screamed those
monstrous two words, "Crucify Him!" Not the soldiers, for
they were under orders when they nailed Christ to the
cross. All had a part in the guilt of the crucifixion; no one
in all humanity is innocent of the blood of that just Man.
But the chief responsibiilty for the crucifixion of Christ
falls on him who plotted it. Who wrote the plot? It was a
collaboration, of course, but one man was the leader. If
he could speak for himself, after these years, and would
speak honestly, this is what he might have to say:

When you of the twentieth century place the blame for
the crucifixion of Christ, it is my father-in-law Annas who
usually receives the worst condemnation. You often speak of
him as a fiend. That is what he was. His mind was as

---

[1] Matt. 26:66.
[2] John 19:11.
[3] Matt. 26:15.

sharp as a sword, and as cold and cruel; and where his heart should have been he had a stone.

At the time that the twelve-year-old Christ was asking those amazing questions of the priests in the temple, the religion of Israel (at least among the leaders) was almost dead. The heart had been taken out of it and all that remained was the lifeless form. You would call it formalism. Rome, that ruled my people with an iron hand in a velvet glove, put down Joazar, the high priest chosen by the multitude, and through Quirinius, president of Syria, displaced him with Annas, son of Seth. It was a flagrant violation of the ordinance of God and of the old, established custom of my Church! It was as though the president of your country would appoint the head of your church.

What made the appointment all the more arrant was the fact that Annas was then already an infamous scoundrel. There was no question about his ability; unfortunately all his aptitudes were weighted on the side of evil. He was a politician in the worst sense of the word; that is, he was interested primarily in holding or controlling public office and in using the power of that office for his own personal ends.

For nine years Annas defiled the office of high priest, and when he retired — by special request of Valerius Gratus, procurator of Judea and immediate predecessor of Pontius Pilate—he had developed what you call an organization. He continued to direct the farce from the wings. The fact that he was succeeded by five of his sons (the last one also named Annas, being appointed at the time of Nero) was not a coincidence. I, a son-in-law, was chosen for the high priesthood about the year 18. When the sacred oil was poured abundantly on my head and I put on the high priest's miter with a gold plate bearing the inscription "Holiness to the Lord," Annas was a gray, old fox whose cunning turpitude had grown with the years. He was still active behind the scenes twelve years later, when Christ was put on trial. It is the story of myself, however, that I want to tell.

As a child I, Joseph Caiaphas, was reared in the best traditions of the day. While much of our religion had become a hollow form and a screen for selfish ambitions, we still brought up our children with an emphasis on religious training. That is more than you can say for your age.

For a time I was genuinely interested in religion. Yet when I entered the priesthood to make religion my life's work, I was utterly unspiritual. I would not have admitted my faithlessness at the time, for to be a genuine hypocrite you must at least play the part of sincerity.

The man who occupied the office of high priest should have been a man of outstanding character. The responsibility of the office should have made him better. When I became high priest, I was living a low life, and so shamefully did I abuse my responsibility, that I constantly sank to a lower level. I was deliberately wicked. I did not even seem a saint, and I certainly played the devil.

When I tell you that I was a Sadducee and briefly explain who the Sadducees were, you should know me better and should understand more clearly why I acted as I did. Our religion was a practical infidelity. We were the rationalists of our day, who followed the old principles of Aristotle's philosophy. Every dogma accepted by the fathers was first put through the wringer of our reason with which we squeezed out every thought that had to be accepted by faith. You can imagine what was left. The Bible tells you that we taught "there is no resurrection, neither angel, nor spirit."[4] Other sources will inform you that we denied the all-governing providence of God, insisting that men suffered or prospered by their own hand or by blind chance. Such an attitude did not make us sympathetic to the problems of our fellow men. Naturally, we were not waiting for the Savior; we believed we did not need Him!

You many wonder why a Sadducee like me should have been interested in the office of high priest. Why should I want to be at the head of a church and represent my nation before God? Frankly, on account of what I could get out of it. Having rejected the Law of God which says, "Thou shalt love thy neighbor," I lived according to the law of the Old Adam, "Love and serve thyself."

The office of high priest brought me power. It was a position in which political intrigue flourished like weeds in the fence corner, where everyone sees them but no one disturbs them. I pulled wires and slipped bribes and practiced blackmail in the manner of your worst politicians. I was the most influential man of my people.

The office of high priest brought me wealth. Your modern rackets are not startling compared with what we, the religious leaders, accomplished. We controlled the

---

[4] Acts 23:8.

sale of animals used for sacrifices, putting the prices as high as we dared. We controlled and charged for the examination of all animals that were sacrificed. We controlled the changing of the half-shekel temple tax into temple coin, demanding about 4½ cents for each exchange. Everything necessary for celebrating the Passover could be bought from us. Our annual gross "take-in" was large. The purpose for which it was used was determined by us. Since I was high priest, my voice had special weight. Need I explain how I became a wealthy man?

Do you see how valueless is the mere form of religion? Paul, greatest man in the history of your Church, speaks of "keeping up the forms of religion, but resisting its influence."[5] When the form of Christianity means more to a man than its essence, that man is in danger of becoming what I was. I understand you have examples of it in the church today, especially among those who, like me, have a "professional connection with religion." They may display an admirable zeal in defending the position of their denomination and in their very defense demonstrate that Christ's appeal for love has had no influence on them. Others are more delighted in detecting "heresy" in the belief of another, than they are in the discovery that another believes in the Savior and will spend eternity with them. Christ's hands were open to all the world; there are those in your day who are inclined to close them and make fists out of them. Still others are more concerned about the proper position of the altar candles during worship than they are about the right attitude of the heart.

---

[5] II Tim. 3:5 (A. T.)

Our great sin was not what we did to Christ. Our great sin was what we had become through the years, which made it possible for us to do to Him what we did. You should be able to appreciate how I and my cohorts felt about Christ and His teaching. The Pharisees, our opponents, were waiting for the Messiah. It was my chief duty, as high priest, to announce the arrival of the Savior. Yet, when He came, He did not fit into our religion. What a tragedy! What we had come to stand for, did not harmonize with what God's Son was and said and did. God could not be reconciled with our teachings of God. That is why we killed Him!

Do not be too hasty in condemning us on that score. Many of your contemporaries are guilty of a similar perversion. What they want is a religion that fits their life as it is. Religion must demand no changes in their life; it must require nothing that they are not already doing and it must forbid nothing that they are doing. That is not religion and certainly not Christianity. Christianity changes lives. In your age, when men find that their lives do not conform to the principles of Christianity, instead of changing their lives, too many try to change Christianity. They trim it down to accommodate their own desires and attitudes. They eliminate whatever does not suit their taste. And they still call it Christianity.

I did not discover Christ suddenly, late one Thursday evening, when a mob brought Him to my palace. Coolly and craftily I had arranged for that meeting. Some three years earlier we had sent a delegation to a rugged wilderness preacher, only to have him insult us by calling us a "generation of vipers."[6] He warned us that he would be followed by one far greater and mightier. When the next Passover came, we understood more clearly what he meant.

In the course of the festival a young man appeared in the temple market and single-handed drove out the cattle and those that sold them. He tipped the tables of the money-changers. He sternly commanded the sellers of doves, "Take these things hence; make not my Father's house a house of merchandise."[7] Such presumptuous interference first shocked and then infuriated us. I was all for putting Him out of the way immediately; but even villainy cannot always have its way. There was the crowd to consider.

The problem became more irritating and more vexing, as He began to scorn and denounce us openly with uncompromising indignation, and to perform amazing miracles of all kinds. The crowd that followed Him became larger. At the time there was little we could do but shadow Him. Our men were in the multitude that witnessed His Miracles and heard His sermons. They were constantly bringing in discouraging reports. He was growing in favor with the people. Occasionally we prompted our scouts to ask Him questions, or we ourselves appeared to ask them in the hope that we might incriminate Him. But His perfect insight and indisputable logic were disheartening so that we always came off a poor second-best. What disturbed me most was the impression He was making on the people. His nobility of character emphasized our depravity; His love

---

[6] Matt. 3:7.
[7] John 2:16.

for men of all kinds called attention to our contempt for all who were not of our party; His popularity forcefully reminded us of our unpopularity. Thus it became increasingly evident that we would not be able to live with Him in the same temple, not even in the same country.

The problem took a turn for the worse with the announcement that Christ had raised Lazarus from a grave of four days. Whether the report was true did not immediately interest us. It did disturb us that the people believed it. Something would have to be done quickly. The time of waiting was at an end; the time for action had come!

At a hastily called meeting of the Sanhedrin we were getting nowhere; members were merely re-stating the problem that something would have to be done. I was getting impatient. Without an attempt to hide my disgust, I contemptuously stepped before the council and said, "Ye know nothing at all, nor consider that it is expedient for us, that one man should die for the people, and that the whole nation perish not."[8] The irony almost makes me smile to this day. The thought that I, a temporizing opportunist, should be sincerely concerned about the future welfare of the people was flagrantly ridiculous. It was not the Sanhedrin's want of knowledge, but my utter lack of scruples, that made it possible for me to be the one to suggest the solution. To me it made no difference whether an action was right or wrong; all that mattered was the benefit I derived from it. The Sadducees cannot live peaceably with Christ in the same world—that was my logic—hence, Christ must die.

In spite of all the practical selfishness in my suggestion, I spoke most profoundly. God had said essentially the same

[8] John 11:49-50.

thing, but in a widely different sense. God meant, "It is better that my Son dies, than that all humanity perishes in its sin." That was love unspeakable! I meant, "It is better that this man dies, than that I lose my office." That was despicable self-love!

Then came Palm Sunday. The way the multitude acclaimed Him as it brought Him into our city, frightened us with the realization that the climax was near. If we were going to act, we would have to act speedily and ruthlessly.

On Monday He cleansed the temple again, as He had done three years earlier. This time He even called our temple a den of thieves. As I look back now, it seems as though He was forcing us to act quickly. A gleam of fierce joy shot into my heart when the man Judas came in with the offer to betray Him. If one of His own disciples was not afraid to oppose Him, why should we hesitate? Judas did not think it would be difficult to take Him. We closed the deal with him and then there was no turning back.

How we sent out our men with Judas to take Christ prisoner in the night, you know. You remember also how He was brought to our palace. Did you ever realize that we were not ready for Him? The sentence had been passed, weeks earlier, "He must die." What we still needed was a reason for putting Him to death. It all sounds most absurd now. We were not trying Him to determine what punishment was to follow on a crime He had committed. The punishment had been fixed and what we wanted was a crime of which we could accuse Him to make the punishment appear just! You follow the same false and illogical procedure when you condemn a thing for reasons of personal distaste alone, and then search the Scripture for support in your prejudice.

One of your writers has found 43 "direct and specific violations of civil law" in the arrest, trial, and execution of Christ. No doubt there were many. The opening of the trial failed miserably and succeeded only in demonstrating that our witnesses were deliberately perjuring themselves. For that we should have stoned them. None of our witnesses could agree enough to give the testimony even the semblance of truth. Our time was running short and in sheer exasperation I stepped before Christ to put Him under the most solemn oath. "I adjure thee by the living God, that thou tell us whether thou be the Christ, the Son of God."[9] He had been silent for a time, but an oath of that kind had to be answered. He answered it. It was what I wanted; still I trembled. In effect He responded, "Just as you have said it, I am the Christ." The entire council should have risen immediately to shout in great chorus, "Amen!"

There was a tense silence. I broke it with a most disgusting act. Tearing my clothes in mock sorrow, I shouted, "He hath spoken blasphemy; what further need have we of witnesses? Behold, now ye have heard His blasphemy. What think ye?" They who had refrained from confessing with a great "Amen!" joined their voices in a terrible "He is guilty of death."[10] In the Talmud was written, "The Sanhedrin is to save life, not destroy it." The Sanhedrin became guilty of murder maliciously aforethought.

All night we treated Him shamefully and inhumanely. Reluctantly Rome carried out the death sentence in the morning. We thought we were rid of Christ, who did not fit into

---

[9] Matt. 26:63.
[10] Matt. 26:65-66.

our religion. Then two days after the crucifixion, He was back and we knew we would never be rid of Him.

Something that He said as He stood before me that memorable night keeps tolling in my mind like a great bell, "I am the Son of God. Hereafter shall ye see the Son of man sitting on the right hand of power, and coming in the clouds of heaven."[11]

---

[11] Matt. 26:64.

SIMON

And as they came out, they found a man of Cyrene, Simon by name: him they compelled to bear his cross.—MATT. 27:32.

THE story of Lent is the story of wrong choices. The religious leaders had to choose between the end of their stagnant formalism and the death of Christ. They killed Christ brutally. Judas had to choose between His Lord and thirty pieces of silver. He took the silver greedily. The disciples had to choose between the danger of loyalty and the safety of flight. They fled fearfully. Peter had to choose between confessing Christ and blaspheming Him. He blasphemed shamefully. The mob had to choose between Christ and Barabbas. They clamored for Barabbas fanatically. Pilate had to choose between justice that would rouse the formidable antagonism of the Jews and injustice that would win their momentary favor. Finally he was flagrantly unjust. Practically every character whose part in the Passion Story is written in the Sacred Record, chose evil rather than good. There is one happy exception. One man acted nobly and for nineteen hundred years he has been praised before Christian congregations. But he had no choice. He was compelled to act as he did. Let him tell his own story:

My name is Simon. Like Simon Peter, I was sometimes called Simeon. Once the Bible refers to me as Niger, i.e. "the black one." The name was appropriate for I was tanned dark by the hot sun of North Africa. My home was in Cyrene. You will understand better when I tell you that I lived near the city of Bangazi, where one of the great battles of your current war was fought.

One Friday morning in spring I was on my way to Jerusalem, the center of our Jewish world, to take part in the great Passover Festival. The trip was not unusual. On the day of Pentecost your minister probably reads the passage from the Acts of the Apostles that lists among the visitors in Jerusalem for the Feast of Weeks, dwellers in Mesopotamia, Phrygia, and Pamphylia, in Egypt, and in parts of Libya about Cyrene.[1] Some of you would not walk far to a service, but we thought enough of our God and of our Church gladly to travel more than a thousand miles on camel-back or on foot, at least once a year, to celebrate one of the great festivals in the city of the temple.

Joy ruled the morning as I approached the city of which David sang, "beautiful for situation, the joy of the whole earth."[2] My heart beat high as I saw again from a distance how the sun played on the gilded roofs of the temple and bleached the marble colonnades. Everywhere gay pilgrims were moving toward the gates of the city.

The happy morning song ended abruptly as one of the strings of my heart's harp broke, unexpectedly. A large crowd leaving the city discomposed me when I realized that it was a funeral procession for three men who were about to die. You do not execute men on holidays; the contrast with happy surroundings adds unnecessarily to the tragedy. Here was deep tragedy! My curious glance fell on two of the condemned men. Some one was walking ahead of them with a wooden slate on which was written the nature of

[1] Acts 2 :9-10.
[2] Psalm 48 :2.

their guilt. They were hard men who had lived their lives in defiance of the laws of God and men, and their demeanor on this last mile revealed that they intended to die that way—defiantly.

I looked at the third man. What I saw was impressed unforgettably on my memory. He was an utterly exhausted and thoroughly beaten man. Numerous little, caked streaks of blood marked His pale, unshaven cheeks. The hair around his head was matted with dry blood. His eyes looked in upon a spirit sorely tried and sadly tired. The sight of the white robe covering His back was ghastly. His hands trembled as they clutched the cross. Later I learned what He had suffered: unutterable agony in a garden; a sleepless night of mock trials, ridicule, and torture; the shock of a whipping that would have killed a man of slighter frame. He staggered so badly with the cross that it was evident to all He would be unable to carry it farther.

I looked around for His friends. It seemed strange that no one was ready to help Him. It would have seemed stranger still if I had known about the hundreds of cripples, blind, deaf, lepers, possessed, and even dead, to whom He had restored the full use of their faculties. Where were they? As I surveyed the crowd for a likely candidate to carry the cross, one of the soldiers looked at me and said brusquely, "You carry it!" That settled it! Objection would have been useless. The overspent cross-bearer crawled from under the cross with a look of relief and gratitude. Reluctantly I stooped and took His place. For that I shall be remembered as long as the Bible is read. My only regret is that all who hear my story will know that I was forced to carry the cross.

You have made much of what I did that morning. It was little. Many of you have performed tasks of greater difficulty. Your artists usually picture the cross as a structure of huge beams, and those in some of your most famous paintings would weigh at least 500 pounds. The cross I carried was crudely made and just strong enough to hold the weight of its victim. Any normal man in the crowd could have done what I did. I like to think I am remembered today, not because my action was so outstanding, but because it has become symbolical for the cross-bearing of humanity.

All of you know something about crosses. You understand how tears are made. Many of you are learning hard and fast these days. "Grief walks through the earth," you say, "and sometimes sits at the feet of every man." The cross is like that. God has a great supply of crosses and one of them will fall, late or soon, from one side or another, on every life. Some of you have crosses so small, you are scarcely aware of them; and the sun seems to be shining on all sides of your house. Some of you have crosses so large and heavy, you are wondering whether the sun will ever shine again.

Crosses can come into your life with shocking suddenness, as abruptly as the ringing of the telephone and as unexpectedly as an accident. Mine came that way. It was a beautiful spring morning and the day in the city promised to be one of impressive worship and merry-meeting with old friends. Then came the cross! Never forget, it can come to you like that. Life is quite pleasant and satisfying as you stand over the ironing board, listening to a sentimental drama on the radio, wiping away a tear now and then, smiling because such tears are easily wiped away. Then it comes! Western Union brings news that is the real thing. Tears flow and it does no good to wipe them away. Or, you are driving home from work, making plans for an enjoyable evening. They never materialize. There is an accident and you spend uncomfortable days and nights on a hospital bed. Or, you go to the doctor, confident that you will be well in a day or two, and his verdict falls like a bombshell.

When the cross comes, it can pick you up and set you to live your life along paths you never dreamed of. I was on my way to Jerusalem; but with the cross, I went off in the opposite direction. I was going to celebrate. Instead, I struggled with a burden. I perspired and soiled my clean clothes. I carried an instrument of death, and thought it as revolting as you would the handling of a hangman's noose. I defiled myself ceremonially. How often have you revised your plans because a cross stood in the way? You dream of a family of your own and then discover you will never marry. You plan a career—as a musician, let us say —and an accident takes several fingers. You save for a new home, and sickness eats your savings. The cross changes lives.

I had a great advantage over you. As I walked along the road that morning, I could see little of the cross and I had no one to talk to. Some of you look at almost nothing else in life but your cross, and you keep on talking about it. Some of you preserve the memory of an old affliction on a convenient shelf in your mind and take it down every day or so and nibble at it just to keep going, and you offer some of it to everyone who comes near. You enjoy nothing quite so much as a recital of all your crosses, real or imaginary. If you had married more fortunately, if you had been educated better, if your parents had been more understanding, if you had not been ill, if hard luck were not forever dogging your steps, you would not be of all men most miserable. I say, I had an advantage in that there was no one to talk to about my cross! But you do not have to talk about yours. God has given you so many blessings that were unknown to us. Talk about them for awhile.

The peculiar quality of your cross is not important, but *how* you carry it is important. Somewhere in this great country of yours there lives a woman on whom the Lord has placed a frightfully heavy cross. In the course of two weeks she lost her husband, and her two children, and was herself permanently and painfully crippled. Nevertheless, she is still patient and believing. "If that's what God wants," she says with true Christian resignation, "I want it too." In another part of your country there is a young lady, frustrated and cynical, her faith ground to bitterness. A little scar has come to mar her beauty. "How can God be so cruel?" she sobs. You remember what God once permitted in the life of Job. Poor Job was bent way over under the weight of a monstrous cross. But Job lifted his head long enough to confess, "Though the Lord slay me, yet will I trust in him."[3] How do you carry your cross?

I had another advantage over you. My burden was another's relief and I could see how grateful He was. Later it became clear to me that the wooden cross I carried for Him was insignificant compared with the load of sin He carried for the world, and for me. He carried it for you, too.

---

[3] Job 13:15.

He did not have to do it. He did it because He loves you. Think of that sometime when your cross gets heavy.

In carrying the cross I did something in common with all men. In carrying Christ's cross, I did something in common with all true Christians. It seems strange, does it not, that I should have carried the cross for the Son of God? And yet, it is just as strange that Christ should give you of this latter day an opportunity to carry a cross for Him. The soldiers told me gruffly, "You take the cross!" Christ appeals to you, "Take up your cross and follow me."[4] In fact, He makes the cross an indispensable condition of Christian discipleship, "He that taketh not his cross, and followeth after me, is not worthy of me."[5] By "cross" Christ does not mean the inevitable afflictions to which all flesh is heir. He means the sacrifice and the self-denial and everything you suffer because you are a Christian.

How heavy is your Christian cross? What has it cost you in time and effort, in comfort and contributions, to be a Christian? What do you know about suffering for Christ's sake? Do you know what our Christian faith cost some of us in the early years of the Church's history? We gave up everything earthly, even our lives. We faced not merely the ridicule of a sophisticated world! We faced a vicious enemy who burned us alive or had us torn to pieces by ravenous lions.

A writer of your day complains that you have made Christianity too easy. You never fast, you never abstain from anything, you never deny yourself anything, you never sacrifice in your giving, and you are never ridiculed for

[4] Matt. 16:24.
[5] Matt. 10:38.

your faith because you live too much the way the world lives. If you are a true follower of Christ you will count no sacrifice too great, you will consider no suffering too severe, and you will look upon no hardships as being too difficult.

Now I will say something many of you know and others will find hard to believe. The cross is your greatest blessing in life. It will turn to pure gold if you carry it aright. The cross I carried that morning set my feet on a path that led me to the great, eternal treasure. It took me to Calvary and it was at Calvary that I learned to know, and believe in, the Lamb of God that taketh away the sin of the world.

One of the earliest Christian churches was established at Cyrene. Tradition gives me most of the credit. It makes little difference now how much I had to do with it. But of one thing you may be certain. I had to tell others of the Savior I found on Calvary. I took my family to Calvary and they learned to believe in the Savior. That is why Paul, in writing to the Romans, sends greetings to "Rufus chosen in the Lord and his mother."[6] The Romans knew them as Christians. They were my boy and wife. Because I carried the cross for Christ not I only, but my family also became Christian. It might not have happened if I had come to Jerusalem five minutes later, or by another gate. The cross I was compelled to carry for Christ brought me eternal blessing. Blessed are they who willingly take their cross and follow Christ.

In my later years I frequently sang with the Psalmist,

---
[6] Rom. 16:13.

"Before I was afflicted I went astray: but now have I kept thy word...It is good for me that I have been afflicted; that I might learn thy statutes."[7] Later, too, I understood the writer to the Hebrews, "Discipline is never pleasant at the time; it is painful; but to those who are trained by it, it afterward yields the peace of character."[8]

Learn to say with Thomas Shepherd:

> *Must Jesus bear the cross alone,*
> *And all the world go free?*
> *No, there's a cross for everyone,*
> *And there's a cross for me.*
>
> *The consecrated cross I'll bear*
> *Till death shall set me free;*
> *And then go home my crown to wear,*
> *And there's a crown for me.*

[7] Ps. 119:67, 71.
[8] Heb. 12:11. (A. T.)

THE CENTURION

*Certainly this was a righteous man.—*LUKE 23:47.
*Truly this was the Son of God.—*MATT. 27:54.

IT was a Roman centurion whose unexpected and firm
faith moved Christ to marvel and who won from the
Master the high commendation, "Verily I say unto you, I
have not found so great faith, no, not in Israel."[1] It was a
Roman centurion who is nobly described in the Sacred
Record as "a devout man, and one that feared God with all
his house, which gave much alms to the people, and prayed
to God alway."[2] It was a Roman centurion who glorified
God in the moment of Christ's sublime and edifying death
with a thrilling confession that stands in acute contrast to
the blasphemous ridicule of the heartless spectators on
Calvary and to the cringing silence of Christ's closest followers, when he said: "Certainly this was a righteous man.
Truly this was the Son of God."

A centurion was captain of a century, a division of the
Roman army originally numbering probably one hundred
men. As a Gentile he was usually a stranger to the faith and
hope of Israel. The centurion who stood on Calvary was
leader of the Roman guard and in charge of Christ's execution. If tradition may be trusted, his name was Longinus.
His was a unique experience; after executing a condemned
Man, he was overwhelmed with the conviction that he had
made an enormous mistake, and immediately pronounced his
Victim righteous and divine. The priests had said of the

---

[1] Matt. 8:10.
[2] Acts 10:2.

Man marked for death, "He is guilty of death." The mob had screamed, "Crucify Him!" The Roman procurator had consented to His execution—although under protest, "Take ye Him, and crucify Him." The Roman centurion, however, (unable to restrain himself after what he had seen and felt), defied the priests, the mob, and Rome with a clear and bold confession, "This was a righteous man and the Son of God." He demonstrates how God can reaffirm the truth, even when it has been nailed to a cross! If the centurion could speak to us after all these years and tell of his experience, he might put it like this:

Time marches relentlessly on, more quickly than we know. It seems like yesterday that a command was given to me one Friday morning, "Centurion, crucify these men!" The morning had dawned like any other day in spring. It was to be a great and exciting day. Hundreds of thousands of Jews had come from all parts of the world to celebrate their annual Passover Festival. Special soldiers had been detailed to help keep order in the city. We had heard that during the night a strange trial had been held by the Jewish court and that Pilate would be compelled to ratify and carry out a sentence of death on an innocent man or face revolt. The rumor was true. It was simple to predict Pilate's course of action. Under pressure a weak character will be selfish and unfair. Pilate was outrageously unjust. Although he insisted to the very end that the Man was innocent, he actually gave permission to crucify Him.

The Victim of Jewish hatred and Roman injustice was not a total stranger to me. I had heard of Him, "The Prophet of Nazareth." For three years He had been traveling throughout Palestine, calling sinners to repentance, forgiving the penitent, blessing the children, cheering the discouraged, comforting the bereaved, healing the sick, raising the dead. His life had been lived in terms of love and sacrifice. A man in my position, however, was not supposed to be what you call a religious man. When my companions spoke of Him, they did it jokingly. Now He had only a few hours to live. It was the privilege of my earthly life and the salvation of my eternal life, that I was very close to Him during those last hours.

"Centurion, crucify these men!" Two others were to be crucified with the Innocent—criminals of the blackest stripe. Many visitors would witness or hear of the execution, and my government never missed an opportunity to strike fear in the heart of all who were inclined to break Roman law.

"Centurion, crucify these men!" The command was not unusual. Ghastly scenes and brutal assignments were part of my business. I was a true soldier. By repeated contact with the inhuman my heart had become hard and was not easily touched by fear or pity. What I did not know was that God can go right through the calluses on a man's heart and touch it where it will respond. That day I was to learn that God can in a moment frighten the boldest and most defiant of men and let them know that He is God whereas they are only men. One of your soldiers in the Southwest Pacific, trained to "take it," wrote with more feeling than poetic skill:

> *Look, God, I have never spoken to you;*
> *But now at last I will be true.*
> *Last night from a shellhole I saw your great sky;*
> *I figured right then they had told me a lie.*

Had I taken time to see things you had made,
I'd have known the truth they would have me evade.
I wonder, God, if you'd shake my hand?
Somehow I feel that you'll understand.
Funny I had to come to this hellish place
Before I had time to see your face.
Well, I guess there isn't much more to say;
But I'm sure glad, God, I met you today.
I guess the "zero hour" will soon be here.
But I'm not afraid, since I know you're near.
The Signal! Well, God, I'll have to go.
I trust you deeply, that I want you to know.
You realize well this will be a horrible fight!
Who knows, I may come to your house tonight.
I wonder, God, if you'd wait at the door.
Look, I'm crying! Me sheddin' tears!
I wish I had known you these many years.
Well, I'll have to go now. God, good-bye!
Strange, since I met you, I'm not afraid to die.

"Centurion, crucify these men!" It was about nine o'clock
in the morning when I received the command. We were
ready with the implements of torture. From the beginning
it was evident that this crucifixion would be different from
any I had ever performed. It was the Innocent One who
made the difference. Others about to die had usually been
defiant or cowardly; He was calm and confident. Others
had been vindictive; He was kind and forgiving. How grateful He was when we relieved His beaten body of the heavy
cross! How sorrowful He was when He had to warn the
weeping women of the impending doom of their city! How

brave He was when He refused the benumbing drink provided by the wealthy ladies of Jerusalem! How composed and submissive He was when we nailed Him to the cross! His exhausted body stretched over the rough wood lying on the ground—the open palms that had often blessed, but had never hurt—the sharp iron spikes—the lifted mallet—no, I must not! A true picture of the crucifixion would make all of you shudder and some of you faint. I can still hear the haunting sound of the mallet blows.

Others, as they were being crucified, had often rent the air of Calvary with their shrieks of pain and their screaming to heaven for vengeance on their tormentors, or had made it blue with their dreadful oaths; but He was silent. When finally He did speak, in a moment of agonizing pain, it was to pray calmly; not for Himself, but for us, His pitiless murderers, "Father, forgive them; for they know not what they do." That tore to shreds my soldierly indifference. Have you ever come upon someone who was praying for you and did not know that you could hear—a parent perhaps, or a friend? One of your contemporaries tells of such an experience. "The most deeply impressive and influential moment of my life," he calls it. Can you appreciate how I felt? The Man I was killing, was praying for me. Here was something not human; it was divine! Others have done likewise, I know; but they had His example and were imitating the divine.

"Father, forgive them." My men probably did not even recognize it as a prayer, much less grasp its significance. They sat down to gamble at the foot of the cross, more interested in the clothes of the Man they killed than in the Man. The coarse-hearted crowd, morbidly curious in the gruesome, was so intent on ridiculing Him, that it did not hear His response.

The behavior of the mob was shocking. Most disgusting of all was the conduct of the priests and Pharisees. They had come, not to console the Dying, but to taunt Him. They forgot entirely the dignity of their office, and celebrated their collusive victory with malignant satisfaction. One could hardly blame the people, the soldiers, and the malefactors for joining them in their devilry. The false accusation voiced before Caiaphas was taken up as the theme of their mockery, "Thou that destroyest the temple, and buildest it in three days, save Thyself."[3] His claim to divinity became the basis of their derisive request, "If Thou be the Son of God, come down from the cross."[4] His holy benevolence was made the butt of their fiendish malevolence, "He saved others; Himself He cannot save."[5] Throughout, the noble Christ remained silent.

Then God spoke. The Pharisees and Sadducees had often asked for a sign from heaven. Now they got it! As noon approached, the bright sun was looking down on the scene of horror. Then it happened! The sun began to hide. It became frightfully dark. For three hours men had been ridiculing the Son of God; for three hours God answered with silent darkness. I remembered having heard that there had been bright light and angel song over the fields of Bethlehem on the night when Christ was born. There was darkness and an awful stillness over the fields of Jerusalem on the day when Christ was killed. The mockery ceased.

---

[3] Matt. 27:40.
[4] Matt. 27:40.
[5] Mark 15:31.

Men moved slowly and spoke in whispers. It had been a terrible place for Him; now it was terrible for us.

Suddenly He called into the darkness, "My God, My God, why hast Thou forsaken Me?"[6] He asked for a drink and received it. He called out a word of triumph and victory, "It is finished."[7] Then He died, like a child falling asleep in the arms of its father, saying confidently, "Father, into Thy hands I commend My spirit."[8]

There were more signs from heaven. The earth shuddered. The rocks burst. Graves opened. Saints arose. The announcement was whispered excitedly that the rich and colorful temple curtain, sixty feet wide and thirty feet high and four inches thick,—the Jews had been so proud of it—had been torn from top to bottom. The darkness had sobered the emotionally upset multitude. These added signs helped them see that a terrible crime had been committed on Calvary—and that they had had a part in it. God had frightened them, too, and had made them know that He is God and they were only men,—sinful, little men. Deeply moved they began to leave Calvary, beating their breasts and wringing their hands.

I could no longer keep silent. The innocence of His life, the nobility of His patience, the sublimity of His heroism, the majesty of His suffering, the divinity of His forgiveness, the infinity of His love, the peace of His dying, the triumph of His death, and the unmistakable signs from heaven impelled me to make a confession, "Certainly this was a righteous man. Truly this was the Son of God." I had

6 Matt 27 :46.
7 John 19 :30.
8 Luke 23 :46.

never studied theology. I had never heard the arguments for His divinity. Yet it was all so clear to me, and so convincing. He *was* the Son of God. He Himself had said it and, righteous man that He was, He could not have lied.

"Certainly this was a righteous man. Truly this was the Son of God." Later I discovered that my confession was not new. To His mother the angel had announced, before His conception, "Thou shalt conceive...and bring forth a Son...He shall be great, and shall be called the Son of the Highest."[9] At His baptism a voice from heaven had said, "This is My beloved Son, in whom I am well pleased."[10] To His question, "Whom say ye that I am?" Peter had responded, "Thou art the Christ, the Son of the living God."[11]

"Certainly this was a righteous man. Truly this was the Son of God." I was not the last one to make that confession. After all these years, millions are confessing it every day. "I believe in Jesus Christ, God's only Son." You have probably repeated it yourself, far more often than you can remember.

"Certainly this was a righteous man. Truly this was the Son of God." I felt what I confessed. Your confession, as you recite the Creed, may be no more than the repetition of memorized words, like the signing of an old form letter whose contents have been forgotten. Your confession ought to be as fresh and sincere as mine. I was standing by the side of Christ when He died, but you have the story of the resurrection and nineteen centuries of evidence to support your confession.

---

[9] Luke 1:31, 32.
[10] Matt. 3:17.
[11] Matt. 16:16.

"Certainly this was a righteous man. Truly this was the Son of God." I returned to Jerusalem that evening far different from what I had been when I had left the city that morning. I could never forget what I had seen and heard. I wanted to know more about Christ. I learned the most glorious truth of all. He is my Savior. I helped to kill Him; but He died for me. John Newton seemed almost to read my thoughts when he wrote what may well be my greater confession:

> *In evil long I took delight,*
> *Unawed by shame or fear,*
> *Till a new object struck my sight,*
> *And stopped my wild career:*
> *I saw one hanging on a tree*
> *In agony and blood,*
> *Who fixed His languid eyes on me,*
> *As near His cross I stood.*
>
> *Sure never till my latest breath*
> *Can I forget that look:*
> *It seemed to charge me with His death,*
> *Though not a word He spoke:*
> *My conscience felt and owned the guilt,*
> *And plunged me in despair;*
> *I saw my sins His blood had spilt,*
> *And helped to nail Him there.*
>
> *Alas! I knew not what I did!*
> *But now my tears are vain:*
> *Where shall my trembling soul be hid?*
> *For I the Lord have slain!*

A second look He gave, which said,
"I freely all forgive;
This Blood is for thy ransom paid;
I die, that thou mayst live."

Thus, while His death my sin displays
In all its blackest hue,
Such is the mystery of grace,
It seals my pardon too.
With pleasing grief, and mournful joy,
My spirit now is filled,
That I should such a life destroy,
Yet live by Him I killed!

I, PONTIUS PILATE

I, PONTIUS PILATE, Governor of the Imperial Province of Syria from 26 to 36 A.D., would like to say a few words to my intellectual and spiritual contemporaries of the twentieth century. If you ask the reason, I can only point to my increasing importance in all the years since that memorable Friday morning when the world's hourglass was turning and I was one of the grains of sand within it. Beyond that there is no good reason why I, of all men, should speak to you. In life I was never very important; merely a minor official in a great colonial empire for a few tragic years. My term of office was marred by continuous rioting. I had nothing but contempt for the fanatic, feverish Jews, constantly bickering and feuding. You may remember that I tried to set the eagles of Rome on the walls of the Temple of Jehovah, but was compelled to remove them after five days. I resolved to build an aqueduct with temple money, and they forced me to abandon the project. Now after all these clarifying years I am ready to admit that in the world of time and power I was a failure.

Nevertheless, it pleases my Roman sense of irony that I should now have become the most famous Roman of them all. When Caesar and Seneca, and Cicero and Tiberius are forgotten, I will be remembered. The Virgin Mary and I are the only human beings mentioned in your Christian creed. Day after day, century after century, millions of human beings have shouted and whispered: "He suffered under Pontius Pilate." Sometimes I wonder if this is not the ultimate irony in history. To my amazement I find myself

famous because early one Friday morning I was face to face
for five or six hours with One Who was greater than I,
Whom I sent to a cross, and Who in return gave me a
reluctant and hateful immortality. I, who would have nothing to do with Him in life, am now linked to Him forever.
Seldom has your unpredictable God turned the normal
course of events more sharply to His own good purposes.

But let me tell you the story of that Friday morning as
I saw it from the judgment seat. You may remember that
in all the imperial provinces of Rome we had kept the right
of review and final decision in all capital crimes. This was
merely a matter of good administration. Ordinarily we were
ready and willing to rubber stamp the decisions of the native courts, because there was seldom more at stake than a
single life. An individual is never important to empire,
as you of the twentieth century well know. That morning,
however, there was something else in the air. Almost immediately I became interested in the case. You have a saying that one should judge a man by his enemies. This man
had the right enemies; in fact, they were mine, too. I was
drawn to Him because the right people were against Him.
Then there was also His royal bearing and His mysterious
indifference to the howling of the mob and the shadow of
death over him. You may consider me a coward or a hard,
cruel man, but you cannot call me stupid. I knew this Friday morning that there were currents and cross-currents beneath the surface of the scene before me which raised it
above the ordinary dramas of crime and punishment. That
was why I did a very strange thing for a judge and almost
immediately called Him innocent. I tried to find a way to
let Him go, but there was no chance of that. The mob

and those fanatic priests! When religion goes wrong, it goes very wrong. I was up against a religious hatred, a religious mania for blood, a religious pride. I ran head-on into the ultimate evil, the perversion of religion for the purposes of darkness.

Then an amazing thing happened. I asked the prisoner, somewhat sarcastically, I must admit, "Art Thou the King of the Jews?", and He took the whole trial from my hands and lips and lifted it up and away from the momentary and the personal into the eternal and the spiritual. At that moment I had to meet the Galilean on the highest level I could reach. Your man Spengler has said that this was the most amazing and dramatic meeting of minds in all history. He was right. Suddenly we became the living symbols of two worlds, face to face as the sun rose over Jerusalem on a Friday morning. The world of power and the world of love! The world of pride and the world of humility! The world of doubt and the world of truth; the world of evil and the world of good! Two types of souls, two ways of life, two worlds, forever separate, forever at war were suddenly face to face. My judgment seat became a battleground and a confessional.

I must admit I felt something of that. My conversation shows it. I tried hard to keep up with the height and depth of the drama in which I was playing. But, you may ask: "Why did you not let Him go?" Well, I almost did. As the hours wore on toward the final scene, the mob troubled me less and less. The Tenth Legion would have been able to handle the situation. There was, however, one man in the crowd who understood me. He knew how my mind worked. His name was Caiaphas. At the critical moment, when everything hung in the balance, he cried: "If thou let this man go, thou art not Caesar's friend." That got me. My enemies lined up with my ambitions and I was lost. How often has that not happened since that Friday morning! A man has a secret fault, a hidden weakness, and his friends or enemies find it, use it—and he crashes. Suddenly I saw myself summoned to Rome and condemned to exile or to death. My career and my life were at stake. It was His life against mine.

And so I decided. Wrongly, you say? Forgive me, but many of you of the twentieth century have given up my prisoner for less than that, for a moment of sin, an hour of price or passion, a bit of money or comfort, the worship of reason. You may throw stones at me if you will; but your hands ought to be clean when you pick them up.

At that moment then I set my feet on the road to everlasting fame and to eternal shame. I must confess that for a moment I shivered in the warm morning sun. Are you interested in my career after that fateful morning? I stayed in Judea three more years and then—the bitter irony of it—what I had feared on that Friday morning came to pass anyway. I was recalled, exiled to Gaul, and committed suicide. Of the many legends which have grown up around me, the only one which is true in its essential meaning is told by Swiss peasants. They report that on stormy nights, when the thunder and lightning play over Mount Pilatus, they can see me washing my hands. I am sure that your poet Shakespeare was thinking of me in the scene in which Lady Macbeth tries to wash her hands of the indelible red of blood:

Out, damned spot! Out I say!—
Here's the smell of blood still!
All the perfumes of Arabia will not sweeten this little
    hand.

I know what she means: I hope you will never know. The desperate attempt to chloroform the soul, to forget the past, to run away from gibbering ghosts that walk with you forever.

Although I have no desire to defend myself so late in the time of man, there is one false impression which I would like to correct. Some of your writers seem to feel that I quickly forgot those five hours with your God. Anatole France, for example, in his "Mother of Pearl" describes a conversation which I supposedly had with a young man many years later. This man is speaking about the Galilean. He tells me that I must have been governor when He was crucified. According to Anatole France I make every effort to recall the case, but finally admit that I do not recall the name. That is not true. I never forgot Him. In fact, I cannot see how anyone who has ever come face to face with Him can quite forget Him. You may reject Him as I did, but you cannot ignore Him. You may send Him off to some Herod of your own, but He will always come back again. You may bend your head over your own dark basin of water, but when you look up, He will still be standing at the door of your heart, quiet and uncompelled, silent and inevitable. This you must learn from me. There is no getting away from Him. Your own century has tried to rid itself of Him in the noise of war, the wine of pleasure, the pride of reason, but He will always come back, either in mercy or in judgment. In your case the latter has happened.

I feel very close to the twentieth century. Since I was reared in the religion of Rome, out of which all life and reality had vanished, I became an agnostic, like so many of you, my friends of the twentieth century. "What is truth?" I said. That was a rhetorical question for me. I thought I knew that there was no such thing as truth; only myths, the creations of the minds of men, wild guesses at the riddle of the universe and of life. What difference did it make what a man believed? I see all this in your century and I feel very modern and very sad. There is really nothing new under the sun; the same mistakes, the same blindness, the same desperate efforts to do the impossible, to get away from God, to dismiss the inevitable Christ, to close the windows of your soul and to pull the curtains against the Eternal.

For a long time after that Friday morning I did not sleep very well. One day I arranged to hear Gamaliel, the great teacher of the Jews, who was lecturing in Jerusalem at the time. As I entered his home he was reading from one of their prophets—Isaiah, I believe his name was—"He is despised and rejected of men; a man of sorrows, and acquainted with grief. He was wounded for our transgressions, he was bruised for our iniquities; the chastisement of our peace was upon him; and with his stripes we are healed." For a moment I wondered. The face of the Galilean, covered with the pain of time and the glory of eternity, loomed before me. Was this the man of that Friday morning? If it was, yours is a very wonderful religion. It would seem that under the shadow of the Cross to which I sent Him, there is room for everyone, no matter how evil or how good. Perhaps even, I thought, for me! But, no, for me it is too late.

DISMAS

OUR speaker this evening is one of the nameless immortals in the history of the human race. He is important only because he typifies an area of human experience, a certain truth, certain lessons which our forgetful age must learn all over again. Despite the fact that his name is known to us only by tradition, he has a right to speak in a Christian church. His significance rests in his universality. As we listen to him we hear the voices of nameless and forgotten millions who bear the real burdens of the world. They are the really important men and women in human history. Their mistakes and tears are our own. They carry significant lessons also for us.

Our speaker is known in the history of the Church as the good thief or the penitent thief. Tradition has it that his name was Dismas. Ecclesiastical calendars have set aside March 25th as his day. About twenty years ago there was a remarkable revival of interest in him created largely by a Chicago journalist. During the past ten years several churches, all of them within prison walls, have been named after him. That is about all we know of Dismas except—and it is a heavenly exception—for the fact that one day about noon he said nine words to God on a Cross which sum up everything that the human heart can ever say to the Eternal. They bring Heaven nearer than the sound of a whisper in a quiet room. Let us listen attentively as Dismas speaks:

I do not imagine that you of the twentieth century are very much interested in my life. Certainly I should not trouble you with the details. Let me just tell you a few things which are so universal that there must be someone in this church to whom my experience may be of value, either as a warning or as an example.

You know me only as a dying man on a cross. You must remember, however, that there were many years before that Friday afternoon. As I look back upon them, I should like to tell you that it was very easy for me to go wrong. Like everything else in life, the journey into evil is a gradual process. It does not come suddenly. Step by step I went down into darkness, and the first step was the hardest. When I committed my first crime I was frightened but I soon got over that. It was so easy! It was easy to live outside the law, to get by with things, to regard myself as the great exception to the law of crime and punishment. Others, I knew, had been caught, but I was sure that I would escape. Somehow, I believed, I would get by. I was the special case to whom the rules of life did not apply. That was my first mistake.

Then came my second error. Because I got by with *doing* wrong I began to *think* wrong. You believe that action follows thought. It is well to remember that action often precedes thought. Because we *do* wrong we begin to *think* wrong. Here, I suspect, I come very close to the twentieth century, especially to the younger generation. I thought I was free to do as I pleased. Nobody was going to tell me what to do. No parents, no law, no God were going to control my actions. I thought, as your whole world of the twentieth century thinks; that freedom meant the right to violate all the laws of God and man; that I could live as I pleased; that I was free to go after all the money I could get, all the pleasure I could find and all the power I could reach.

And—this is my tragedy—I continued to think that until the very last minute. During my entire trial I was still hopeful. Something had always happened when I was in trouble. Surely it would happen this time, too. When the judge pronounced the word "guilty," and when they dragged me out to the hill beyond the gates, I was still hoping against hope. Surely there would be a last minute reprieve! Something would happen to save me.

Something did happen! They laid me down on a cross, took my right hand, placed it on the cross-beam and started to drive a nail through it. With the first flash of blinding, tearing pain I knew I was through. This was the end! Suddenly I saw my life, now and at last, in one piece. The nail was tieing things together. I saw all that I might have been and all that I had become. I saw the shame, the folly, the failure, the futility of my years. This was, as you say in the twentieth century, the pay-off! The drops of blood from my hands and my feet and the feverish agony of creeping death were the last result of my faithless years.

This is my story until nine o'clock on that Friday morning. Are you interested in its meaning? Your pastors, I understand, are taught to preach the Law and the Gospel. Well, this is the Law! The soul that sinneth it shall die! The scales of justice may be off balance for a long time but they always return to normal again. God may not balance His books every day, but in the end He always does. You can get by with many things for many days but in the end life and time and God catch up with you. They are all moving in one direction together and there is no getting away from them under the sun of the unheeding sky. This is the Law!

I hope you will not think that I am telling you this in order to frighten you into leading a good life. Fear is a poor and rotten foundation for goodness. That is why your pastors tell you that the Law cannot save anybody. I know that now. I am telling you all this only because I would like to have you understand clearly what happened to me on that Good Friday. Unless you begin to feel my desperation and my loneliness, the utter hopelessness of my stricken soul, you will not be able to follow the events of the next three hours.

Three of us were hanging on three crosses standing sharp against the blue sky of an April morning. Some of you have learned in these days of pain and separation and tears that the human heart and body can accustom itself to almost everything. After the first sharp, stabbing pain of the nails had become steady and before the last fever had begun, I had a chance to look around. It struck me that this was not the usual crowd which gathered at crucifixions to indulge in the black human impulse which seems to take pleasure in the suffering of others. Outwardly this crowd seemed to be of a higher type. Some important looking people were there. I saw some priests, Scribes and Pharisees. I noticed, too, that they paid no attention to us but were concentrating on the Cross in the center. That interested me. I shook my head to clear away the fog of pain. I heard them cursing, jeering and mocking. They seemed to have a personal, bitter hatred for the Man on the Cross in the center. Apparently they considered His suffering a personal triumph for themselves. The crowd, I suddenly saw, was a mob, a yelling, jeering, inhuman, single animal, a snarling brotherhood of hate.

With a tremendous effort I turned my head and looked at the Man on the Cross in the center. I was curious about Him. Then something happened! Please do not ask me exactly what it was. It has happened a million times since that Friday morning and no one has yet been able to explain it in human terms. "For those who believe in God no explanation is necessary; for those who do not believe in God no explanation is possible." All I know is that I saw in Him the exact opposite of everything that I was and everything that I believed. I saw in Him a goodness which I did not believe existed in my cynical world, the measureless dignity of suffering power, the quiet waiting for a victorious end.

My eyes turned upward to the inscription above His thorn-crowned head: "Jesu Nazarenus, Rex Idaeorum." Suddenly I knew that that inscription was true. Somebody had inadvertently stumbled on the truth. He was a King! He was a King in exile going home, brave banners down, a suppliant from pain, and yet a King Whose Kingdom, I thought, would be a wonderful place to live, a land of peace, joy and glory.

For a moment, I must admit, I thought of asking Him to take me when He would be ready to go, but I dismissed that thought immediately. There was no chance of that. Heaven after a life like mine? I, Dismas, in the company of angels and archangels? No, that was too much to hope. I knew I had no future and no chance. I was getting what was coming to me. The thing to do, I thought, was to take it and die.

And yet I wanted to say something to Him. I wanted Him to know that I believed in Him. I wanted Him to know that I knew that He had a future, that He was not going to die without hope as I was dying, that for Him the rest was not silence but song and life and victory. I wanted Him to know that He had a friend in the crowd who would be more than satisfied with anything that He might want to give.

And so, you will recall, I turned to Him and whispered: "Lord, remember me when Thou comest into Thy Kingdom!" I knew it was a small thing and a great thing to ask, beyond tears and beyond time, the old, old human cry, the longing never to be stilled in heaven in a heart like mine, that somewhere and sometime, when life is done someone might remember us, think back to us, and pay to our fading memory the tribute of a passing thought. I did not want to be forgotten!

You remember what happened then. He turned and looked at me; "Today"—the word fell on my heart confident and triumphant, unshadowed by any doubt or fear. I knew I would be with Him forever. He gave me more, infinitely more, than I had asked. That night we came to the gates of Paradise. King and thief, the judge and the sinner, God with His man and man with his God! We who had met at the crossroads of our ways of sorrow went on beyond the sunset into a new and eternal morning. I was redeemed!

That is your religion. That is your faith. That is your hope. If you have seen that, you need not be afraid of anything. In life or in death you are safe. Better than I, you Christians must know today that He will always be with you. I ask you to join me in saying to Him:

> *"Thy arms will strengthen me; and I know*
> *That somehow I shall follow when you go*
> *To the still land beyond the Evening Star*
> *Where everlasting hills and valleys are*
> *And evil shall not hurt me anymore*
> *And terror shall be past, and grief and war."*

I learned that at three o'clock one Friday afternoon and it is still a wonderful thing to know.

PAUL

And last of all he was seen of me also, as of one
born out of due time.—I Cor. 15:8.

WHAT a host of men are this morning delivering sermons on the Easter theme! It has been an annual oc-
currence for almost 1900 years. Who of all the several million New Testament preachers is best qualified to preach
an Easter sermon? Most of us will select the Apostle Paul.
He learned from personal and startling experience what it
means to come suddenly face to face with the risen Christ.
The brilliant strength of his intellect, the eloquence of his
tongue, the facility of his pen, the devotion and charity of
his great heart, combine to make "the happy little Jew who
knew the Lord Jesus Christ better than anyone in all the
world" one of the most richly blessed men of all time. With
the fierce zeal of a misguided conscience he was determined
to use his outstanding abilities to destroy the faith men
had in Christ. Then he met Christ. Instantly he was con-
quered by Him and became the greatest follower Christ ever
had.

Paul was born a Roman and a descendant of Benjamin
in the city of Tarsus, chief city of Cilicia, about the time
"God sent forth His Son." He gloried in his Roman citizen-
ship and he was proud of his Jewish ancestry. Having been
reared by his parents in faithful observance of Hebrew religion and tradition, he continued his formal education at
Jerusalem. There, in his own words, he was "brought up
...at the feet of Gamaliel," (the most distinguished rabbi of
the day) "and taught according to the perfect manner of the

law of the fathers, and was zealous toward God."[1] Like his father he became an ardent Pharisee, "exceedingly zealous of the traditions of the fathers."[2] He was conversant with the Scriptures of the Old Testament and quoted in his letters from more than 200 verses of it—many scholars believe from memory.

No reasonable man living would dare to presume to preach like Paul. But it is permissible to imagine what the Apostle would say to an Easter audience if he were to preach in the style of a modern Christian minister. His sermon might be something like this:

Your Easter Festival amazes and puzzles me. The hundreds of years that lie between your day and mine have brought significant changes not only in standards and modes of living, but in church observances as well. You have made of Easter practically a national holiday in which all take part, Christian and pagan. Were I to attend only an Easter service, I would be immeasurably thrilled by the number of worshippers. But your enthusiasm is so momentary. One of your preachers has called Easter "America's annual religious spasm." The Sunday after Easter you have appropriately named "low Sunday."

I wish you could have taken part in one of the early Easter Festival services. The number of worshippers was small. The place of meeting was a closely guarded secret. But the spirit and the devotion displayed there would have put all of you to shame. Where did you get the name "Easter"? It was called "The Desirable Day of Salvation." The greeting for that day was "The Lord is risen," and the

---

[1] Acts 22:3.
[2] Gal. 1:14.

response was, "He is risen indeed." And where did you get the customs? If I were to ask your children what Easter is, many would probably answer, "That's the day we all go to church—for a change, wear new clothes, and eat colored eggs." There was a day when the children were told that the eggs were a symbol of the tomb of Christ, which was sealed but still contained life. And the eggs were usually colored red as a reminder of the blood of Christ, shed to make Easter possible. It is one of the tragedies of your day that for many of you Easter has come to mean little more than "a new hat and let's hope it doesn't rain."

Let me tell you what the Day of Resurrection came to mean to me. The first Easter was past. The leaders of my church had regarded Christ as highly dangerous to our religion and with bitter fanaticism had put Him to death on a dark Friday. But that was not the end. Everyone heard that Christ had risen from the dead on Sunday morning. According to stories that were whispered everywhere the Roman soldiers guarding the tomb had been frightened to a faint by an angel who rolled away the stone revealing that the tomb was empty; the angel had told all who came to the tomb that Christ had risen according to His promise; the risen Christ had repeatedly appeared to His followers. I never dreamed the stories were true.

We Pharisees had killed Christ to be rid of Him. We were determined that anyone who confessed to believe in His resurrection should publicly be forced to blaspheme Him, or likewise die. When men have set their mind, any evidence that they are wrong will usually drive them more furiously to defend their error.

It is my great shame that I took a leading part in persecuting the Christians. Even my good friend Luke could not keep my part in the nefarious work out of the Sacred Record. He wrote where all men can read: "As for Saul, he made havoc of the church, entering into every house, and haling men and women, committed them to prison."[3] Later when I was thrown out of the temple by the riotous multitude which was set upon killing me, I confessed that I had been guilty of the same crime: "I persecuted this way unto death, binding and delivering into prisons both men and women."[4]

There came the day we stoned to death noble, young Stephen of irresistible wisdom and spirit. (How I could have used him in my mission work!) So vicious was our persecuting that we succeeded in taking prisoner or driving from Jerusalem all members of the Christian Church, except the Apostles. Not content with forcing the Christians to leave the city, I obtained permits from the high priest to go to Damascus, 150 to the northwest, and take prisoner any of Christ's disciples I could find. Since their teaching was contrary to what I regarded as the truth of God, I never doubted that my work was pleasing God.

It was on my way to Damascus, as I was approaching the great and beautiful city, that I met the risen Christ. The story is written three times in the Book of Acts. Let me repeat what I once told Agrippa: "On the road at noon, I saw a light from heaven brighter than the sun flash around me and my fellow-travelers. We all fell to the ground, and I heard a voice say to me in Hebrew, 'Saul! Saul! Why do you persecute Me? You cannot kick against the goad!'

---

[3] Acts 8 :3.
[4] Acts 22 :4.

'Who are you, sir?' said I. The Lord said, 'I am Jesus, whom you are persecuting. But get up and stand on your feet, for I have appeared to you for the express purpose of appointing you to serve me and to testify to what you have seen and to the visions you will have of me. I will save you from your people and from the heathen, to whom I will send you to open their eyes and turn them from darkness to light and from Satan's control to God, so that they may have their sins forgiven and have a place among those who are consecrated through faith in Me."[5]

That moment set in motion a tremendous revolution in my life. The Christ we Pharisees had crucified and whose followers I was killing was alive and speaking with me! The stories about the resurrection were true! He was the Son of God! I had been rebelling against the true and living God! No man had ever made a more damning mistake. And no man ever felt more keenly the love and forgiveness of God. He picked up my life that was being lived in diametrical conflict with His will and turned it completely around. Here was conversion in the truest sense. Saul, the persecuting Pharisee, was dead; Paul, the preaching Christian, had just been born. Here was regeneration in the fullest sense.

To many in your age it all sounds ridiculous, I know, and unbelievable. My experience has been called "the imagination of a weak mind," "an hallucination," "an epileptic fit." You have a habit of giving everything you cannot understand or do not like an uncomplimentary name, thinking that then you are through with it. But you cannot arbitrarily dismiss everything you cannot measure in your scientific

---

[5] Acts 26:13-18 (A.T.).

laboratories; at least not without disastrous results. Life in your day abounds with practical illustrations of that fact. I tell you God was in my experience and you have never made a test tube or a crucible large enough to put God into it. God watches over all your experiments with material things, maintaining natural laws and principles, but you can't experiment with God. If you would accept Christ and His principles for right living with one-third the readiness with which you swallow whole fanciful theories concerning the origin of the world and man, and human panaceas for the betterment of the world, yours would *be* a better world.

Your insistence on scientifically verified knowledge you often bring to church with you, also on Easter Sunday. Some of your preachers make the mistake of trying to prove to you that man is immortal. One of them has listed "six scientific reasons for believing in immortality." But if immortality is a demonstrable fact, it no longer requires any faith to accept it. Others repeat the old analogies on the beautiful butterfly emerging from an unlovely chrysalis and the snow-white lily growing out of an ugly bulb. But they all prove nothing. When someone close to a man's heart has died or when he himself is walking near the outer edge of life, arguments for immortality and analogies on the resurrection are hollow and meaningless. There must be something more personal.

Christ did not try to prove immortality. He spoke of it as He spoke of the existence of God and assumed that men would accept it. "Because I live, ye shall live also."[6] "Who-

---
[6] John 14:19.

soever liveth and believeth in me shall never die."[7] Why not take Christ's word for it? Then you will not need any human argument. If you do not accept Him, no argument will be fully convincing. When He came to me that bright day so long ago, there was nothing for me to do but to surrender to Him completely. "Lord," I asked, "what wilt Thou have me to do?"[8] When you give yourself to Him you need no arguments to bolster your belief in His promises. Truly to know Him and to believe in Him is to trust Him. When sorrow comes or death it will be good to be close to Him. In one of the most trying moments in the life of His followers He comforted them by simply stating, "If it were not so, I would have told you."[9] He never lied; He never deceived anyone; He never made a mistake; His promises have gone into exact fulfillment. He predicted that He would be crucified and promised that He would rise the third day.[10] His crucifixion is an indisputable historical fact. So is His resurrection on the third day.

"If Christ be not risen, then is our preaching vain, and your faith is also vain."[11] In a book written many years ago the author tells of witnessing a European passion play. The audience numbered more than 5000. As the play began, a hush fell on all. When at last the body was taken from the cross and buried, the silence was profound. The little mound on which so many actors had crowded to play the part of the mocking and taunting rabble was suddenly bare. The three crosses stood alone. On the center cross a white cloth flut-

[7] John 11 :26.
[8] Acts, 9 :6.
[9] John 14 :2.
[10] Matt. 20 :19.
[11] I Cor. 15 :14.

tered in the evening breeze. For ten minutes an eloquent silence gripped the vast audience as nothing else in the entire presentation. A question seemed to come to all at the same time. That is why I am telling this. The question was, "Is that the end of the play?" What if it had been? Then the Second Article would end abruptly, "Christ suffered under Pontius Pilate, was crucified, dead and buried." Then the last chapter in the Life of Christ would be on "Death" and it would be a most depressing tragedy. Then Christ, whose influence to this day is stronger and more blessed than that of any man who ever lived, was a cheat. Then the Church, the noblest and most wholesome organization in all history, with all its triumphs over the opposition of evil, is built around a lie. Then Job would have a final "No" to his age-old question, "If a man die, shall he live again?"[12] Then Christians, cherishing the Word and the Sacraments, are "like an infant seeking nourishment from the breast of a dead mother." "Then we are only animated bubbles that rise to the cosmic surface, glisten in the sunlight for a brief space, and then burst, leaving a nasty wet spot on the surface of things."

"But now is Christ risen from the dead."[13] I know, because I saw Him. Think not that I would have given up my life of social prominence and economic security for the life of a man hunted like an animal, beaten, stoned, imprisoned, and finally killed, if the risen Christ had not asked me to do it. I was no fool. I had to make friends of the people I had persecuted. My old friends began to persecute me. Only the phenomenon of learning to know the risen

[12] Job 14:14.
[13] I Cor. 15:20.

Christ and giving myself to Him could have changed me like that.

"But now is Christ risen from the dead." Many others saw Him. During the forty days of His sojourn on earth after His resurrection He appeared to Peter, and to all the Apostles, and to more than 500 of His followers at one time. I discussed it with many of them. I wish you could have heard Peter tell how the Christ whom he had denied and blasphemed appeared to him and reinstated him. He never tired of telling it; often there was a tear of joy in his eye. After the crucifixion the disciples had confessed, "We trusted in Him."[14] On Good Friday their trust had almost died; they were like bruised reeds. But their trust took wings again and soared; they became like sturdy oaks. They staked their lives for time and eternity on the fact that Christ had risen. There is only one explanation for it. They saw the risen Christ.

"But now is Christ risen from the dead, and become the firstfruits of them that slept."[15] In my day the Jewish farmer brought the firstfruits of the harvest to the temple for blessing and sacrifice. It was an earnest that the entire harvest was blessed. Christ, the firstfruit of the resurrection, is God's pledge that the harvest of believers shall also rise. The poet John Oxenham has put the thought into verse:

> *God is! Christ loves! Christ lives!*
> *And by His own*
> *Returning gives*

[14] Luke 24:21.
[15] I Cor. 15:20.

> *Sure proofs of immortality.*
> *The firstfruits He; and we,*
> *The harvest of His victory.*

Death laid hold on Christ and the embrace was fatal for death. Death had been Christ's bitter enemy. Now its stinging power had been removed. Death had been the bitter enemy of God's children. Now it could only serve Christ by bringing His children home. Now Job's question has been answered with a thrilling, "Yes, if a man dies in Christ, he shall live again." Now you need no proof of immortality, you can confidently take up the refrain of Job, "I know that my Redeemer liveth."[16] Now you can sing with Samuel Medley—and mean it:—

> *I know that my Redeemer lives;*
> *What comfort this sweet sentence gives!*
> *He lives, He lives, who once was dead;*
> *He lives, my everliving Head.*
>
> *He lives to silence all my fears,*
> *He lives to wipe away my tears,*
> *He lives to calm my troubled heart,*
> *He lives all blessings to impart.*
>
> *He lives, all glory to His name!*
> *He lives, my Jesus, still the same.*
> *Oh, the sweet joy this sentence gives,*
> *"I know that my Redeemer lives!"*

---

[16] Job 19:25.

May the joy and the peace and the power that was mine when I met the risen Christ, lived with Him, and died in Him, be yours this Easter day and always.

May the glad dawn
Of Easter morn
Bring joy to thee.

May the calm eve
Of Easter leave
A peace divine with thee.

May Easter night
On thine heart write,
"O Christ, I live in Thee."

Meditations on the
Seven Words from the Cross

THE FIRST WORD

"Father, Forgive Them for They Know Not What They Do"
Luke 23:34

O N Good Friday, 1500 years ago, Bishop Ambrose ascended his pulpit in the Cathedral of Milan and addressed his congregation in the following words: "I find it impossible to speak to you today. The events of Good Friday are too great for human words. Why should I speak while my Saviour is silent and dies?" Every preacher of the Cross has had this experience, especially when he compares the weakness of his own words with the majesty and power of the seven short sentences which our Lord spoke in the six hours from nine o'clock in the morning until three o'clock in the afternoon. With these seven words we enter the Holy of Holies of the plans of God for men.

We have come to watch a man die. Because we love Him our watching is hard. We hang upon His last words and carry them in remembering hearts. What does He say Who is now dying for the sin of the world?

"Father, forgive them for they know not what they do." Like lightning His first word strikes directly into the heart of all the troubles of mankind. Once more the weary head goes up under the crown of thorns, a cry echoes out over the crowd, and the world hears a dying man point to the reason for death: "Father, forgive them for they know not what they do." This first word from the Cross echoed back through the long corridors of time. It reached into a garden in the cool of the day. It recalled the dark memory of man's fall and the bright promise: "And I will put enmity between thee and the woman, and between thy seed and her seed, it shall bruise thy head, and thou shalt bruise his heel." This was now the end of that solemn pledge. God was now working out the plan conceived in the garden and worked out in a manger, in another garden and on a Cross. Here was God coming to the hearts of men, calling them by name and bringing them the greatest treasure the heart of God can give—the forgiveness of sins and peace with Him.

Our hurried and forgetful age must see the meaning of this very clearly. Here is the terrible reality of sin. Clearly and definitely! There are a great many things which we can do about sin. We can be sorry for it, we can weep over it, we can regret it, we can offer some small reparation to those who have been hurt by it. One thing, however, we cannot do. We cannot forgive it. This only God can do. Watching with Him under the Cross we hear a voice crying out of the long silences of eternity and over the noise and confusion of 2000 years: "Father, forgive them for they know not what they do."

We have brought memories into this church. Some bless and some burn. There are things in our lives that we should like to forget. Here under the Cross is the washing of your memory and the drying of your tears. Here is relief from the tearing pain in your heart. These words are balm and benediction. When by the mercy of God we believe them, the past is buried in the bottomless sea of the pity of God. "FATHER, FORGIVE THEM FOR THEY KNOW NOT WHAT THEY DO"—here is the beginning of the ascent to Calvary. This is the amazing, humanly impossible miracle of the Cross. This is the miracle of forgiveness, the restoration of fellowship with God, the return to the Father's House. In Him Who died on the Cross our broken heart is healed and our union with God is restored. The great separation, so long and so bitter, has been ended by the reunion with God through Christ. Once more we have the freedom beneath and beyond all human freedoms. Ours is now the great freedom from fear, the freedom from want of God, the freedom of worship of God, the freedom of speech of God. All this—and heaven too—is in the simple words: "FATHER, FORGIVE THEM FOR THEY KNOW NOT WHAT THEY DO."

THE SECOND WORD

"Today Shalt Thou Be With Me in Paradise"
LUKE 23:43

MANY people have been fascinated by the person of the
dying thief. He seems to convey certain lessons to
the modern mind which our age needs bitterly. We can
readily understand that. The story of the thief on the
Cross is the greatest example of the brand snatched from the
burning in the world's history. It is the most magnificent
reflection of the all-embracing love of the Divine Savior.

At Calvary our Lord had come to the cross-roads of the
world and the meeting place of the ages. Here was the
climax of the long years of waiting and preparation. He
was concerned with the sins of all time and all men. He was
suffering for the first and the last sin. Nowhere else is
there a better demonstration of the love of God for the individual human soul than the fact that under these cir-
cumstances He had time to turn to a poor dying thief. This
is the ultimate greatness of the Christian religion; in its last
and highest meaning it places the individual before God
and God before the individual.

"Lord, remember me when Thou comest into Thy Kingdom"—"Today shalt thou be with Me in Paradise." A
strange conversation! Amid the cursing, jeering and howling of the mob there is suddenly a quiet voice: "Lord, remember me." A dying man asks a dying Man to remember.
The answer comes swift and sure, transforming darkness
into light and sweeping over into Heaven a soul for whom

the gates of Hell were yawning wide: "Today shalt thou be with Me in Paradise."

Who was the dying thief? We do not know. He is one of the nameless souls whose history is universal. The story of his life was probably very ordinary. Somewhere along the line he had gotten into bad company, chosen an easy life, and succumbed to the philosophy of getting by. Now he was paying for it, drop by drop of blood from his hands and his feet. This was the end of the road for him.

Suddenly like a stroke of lightning came the voice of his repentance. He knew that the Man on the Cross in the center could save him. There was a way out. He spoke: "Lord, remember me when Thou comest into Thy Kingdom."

The moving humility of his prayer! He does not dare to ask for forgiveness. He says nothing about his possible salvation. Only the single word "remember!" This is the ultimate expression of the old, old human cry, the longing never to be stilled, the deepest need of the human heart. We want someone to remember us even in another world. We do not want to be forgotten. After we are gone we hope that someone will pay us the tribute of a remembering tear and a reminiscent thought.

The tremendous majesty and certainty of the answer! "Today shalt thou be with Me in Paradise." Our Lord turns to him and seems to say: "There will be no waiting for us. We suffered together here. We shall be glorified together there." There is a constant procession of men and women on the road to Paradise. Hour after hour, day after day, year after year men and women begin the long journey to their last home. That night two figures joined the procession, He who had built the road and he who had found it at the end of the way of sorrows. The eternal Son of God was coming home now as His day turned toward evening. He brought with Him a friend. If you want to see how God works; if you want to realize the tremendous power and scope of the Christian faith, look again at this picture! The first soul purchased with the red coin of redemption and marching as the escort of the King of Kings into Paradise, is a poor thief. The first beneficiary of the accomplished atonement is a man who would be in a prison cell today. This is God in His ultimate power and grace!

"Today shalt thou be with Me in Paradise." How often has He whispered these words to a waiting soul since that first Good Friday morning! This morning He has said them to a sufferer on a bed of pain. Perhaps He has whispered them to a business man at his desk. Perhaps their benediction has touched a child at play. Nineteen hundred years ago He said these words in mercy to the dying thief and I pray God He will one day say them in mercy also to us. No more shame and no more sorrow! The same hammers which smote the everlasting doors on Good Friday will open Heaven also for us. The dying Savior and the dying thief will be good company for us here and hereafter.

THE THIRD WORD

"Woman, Behold Thy Son! Behold Thy Mother!"
John 19:26b-27a

SEVERAL young men and women were taking part in a discussion of religion at an institute conducted by a young people's organization. Suddenly a young man in the group said: "It seems to me that very often you preachers talk about things you do not understand." There was much truth in the young man's statement. Ofter the preacher must speak about things which he does not fully understand. In fact, whenever he speaks of God, he is reaching up to the heights and down into the depths of mysteries beyond human wisdom.

This is especially true of the seven words of the Cross. The first two words sweep across heaven and earth, time and eternity. The first marches upward toward heaven and transforms the Cross into the flaming altar of the world's High Priest: "Father, forgive them for they know not what they do." The second transforms Calvary into the vestibule of heaven and the open door to eternity: "Today shalt thou be with Me in Paradise."

The third word, however, remains with us here on earth. It was probably spoken quietly. The Head crowned with thorns was bowed down to the earth where we must live. It is perhaps a little nearer to our full understanding. The feverish eyes of our Lord have searched the crowd for some familiar face. Suddenly he sees a few figures who are near and dear to Him. All except one are women.

For a moment His eyes rest on them and here, at the very center of the world's history, the Son of God becomes once more the Son of Mary. Suspended between earth which had openly rejected Him and Heaven which had seemingly forsaken Him, He remembers His mother, Mary of Nazareth. He bends His head down to her: "Woman, behold thy Son! Behold thy mother!"

All Christian mothers will understand these words better than I. Perhaps Mary's thoughts went back to that silent and holy night when she had first held her Child in her arms. Perhaps she remembered the golden days of His childhood when He grew in grace and wisdom before God and man. Perhaps she remembered Simeon's dark and ominous words: "Yea, a sword shall pierce through thy own soul also." Now she began to understand what he meant. The thorns around the brow of her Son were a circle of flame about her heart. The pain of her motherhood was a sword in her heart. All this He sees from the Cross! He sees the dark and lonely years which lie before her. His whisper comes to her: "Woman, behold thy Son! Behold thy mother."

There are some important lessons for us in this third word from the Cross. Here our Savior reaches down into the small and ordinary things of life. He is making His last will and testament. Here on Calvary with the winds of God's anger sweeping over His soul and all the sorrow of the world centered in His broken heart, He remembers His mother. If this word had never been spoken, we should not have missed it. Our human understanding did not expect it. And yet there it is! In a flash we see the magnificent inclusiveness and universality of the love of God.

It reaches down and away into all problems of life and living. The Christian religion is not only a religion of great churches, chanting choirs, and soaring cathedrals. It is a religion of the home and kitchen, of the little things of life. There is nothing on earth which it does not touch.

On the Cross our Savior remembered His mother. Just so He remembers today the businessman who brings a problem to Him, the housewife who is worried and anxious, the child who holds up a broken finger. His love storms the gates to Heaven and pours itself into every nook and corner of life.

Here is our great and lasting comfort. We may have come to this church worried and anxious. We may have a problem which does not appear important to the world. We may be worrying about something which affects us alone. All these by the magnificent and intimate power of the Cross we can bring to Him who on Calvary remembered His mother. He will remember also us forever!

THE FOURTH WORD

"My God, My God, Why Hast Thou Forsaken Me?"
MATT. 27:46b

SEVERAL years ago the public press reported the story of a man who twenty years earlier had become a victim of amnesia. Known only as Mr. X, he had lived in a small southern town without any memory of his identity. Finally one of our nation-wide radio programs brought him to the microphone to tell his story. At the conclusion of his pitiful tale Mr. X said: "Won't someone please tell me who I am? I do not want to spend my remaining years alone." With these touching words he struck directly into one of the greatest problems of human life, especially in our hurrying and forgetful age—the problem of loneliness! How often does it not appear in our crowded years! "I do not want to spend my remaining years alone!" These words have been spoken in tears, in hidden corners, in crowded cities, and in lonely rooms. There is a deep loneliness in modern life which leaves many of us crying like children in the night. It is a strange fact that despite our great cities and rapid communications, our speed of travel, we are still essentially lonely. The crowds, the speed and the noise are like walls between us. There is no way we can explain the feverish search for company which is often a mark of our twentieth century life. There is no other way to understand the popping corks and clinking glasses of urban living. We are lonely!

When all is said and done, the only answer to our loneliness is the long backward look to Calvary. We must return to Him Who was lonely that we might never be alone. In one sense our Lord's life was the loneliest that was ever lived. He was alone in the desert and on the mountain. He was alone in the crowds that followed Him. He was alone in the garden. He was alone on the Cross. "I have trodden the winepress alone. I am despised and rejected of men."

On Calvary, face to face with the climax of His loneliness, He cries: "My God, My God, why hast Thou forsaken me?" In some strange way known only to God all the timeless sin and shame of the world, wave upon wave, deep calling unto deep, came over Him. He was forsaken of God. It is very difficult for us to understand what happened at that moment. All we know is that this was the ultimate loneliness. This was the only time it ever happened in the long and bitter history of man. A Man was forsaken of God! Let us see this very clearly. No other human being has ever been forsaken of God. No matter how degraded a human soul may become, God is always near. No matter how fast and far it may travel to the dark corners of the world, it is never alone. Here, however, for the first and the last time we come to the last loneliness of the human soul. He is forsaken of God!

There can be only one reason for His loneliness. He was alone that we might never be alone again. He was forsaken of God that we might never be forsaken. He went down into the ultimate depths of sin and shame in order that we might never go down alone. Since Calvary we are never alone. There is always the sound of marching footsteps beside us. There is always a warm hand in ours. There is always company on the road. He bore the terror of the ultimate loneliness in order that in life and death, in youth and age, in joy and sorrow we might never be forsaken of God.

This is our greatest hope and joy. Today we can turn to Him and pray with the faith of a child lost in the dark: "O God my King and my Savior, bow down Thine ear so that through the voices of angels and archangels Thou mayest hear the pleading whisper of a lonely soul:

'Hold Thou Thy cross before my closing eyes,
Shine through the gloom, and point me to the skies.
Heavn's morning breaks, and earth's vain shadows flee;
In life, in death, O Lord, abide with me!' "

THE FIFTH WORD

"I Thirst"
JOHN 19:28b

IT IS probable that the last three words from the Cross were spoken in rapid succession. The warm afternoon was wearing on. The scene had become more quiet. The crowd had been awed into silence by the mysterious noon-day darkness and the strange words of the Man on the Cross in the center. The Roman soldiers looked on with indifference, glad that the whole mean business would soon be over.

Suddenly our Lord raises His head again and we hear the first and last reflection of His physical suffering. "I thirst!" The fourth word from the Cross had been the echo of the deep suffering of His soul. The fifth word is a cry from the suffering of His body.

Once before He had spoken these words: "I thirst!" He had said them long ago to a woman at a well in Samaria. He had told her of the Living Waters which would never fail. Now He was bringing them to the world. By the thirst of His body He was quenching the thirst of human souls.

The human race should not be very proud of its response to His cry. Someone took a sponge, wet it with vinegar, and held it to His lips. Perhaps it was better than nothing! At any rate, it was the world's last offering to its dying Savior. Humanity carelessly brushing the lips of its God with vinegar!

It is tremendously important for us to see the full meaning of His cry. It reflects His complete and full humanity. "For we have not an High Priest which can not be touched with the feeling of our infirmities." He knows them all. He knows every touch of pain, every pang of hunger, every longing for water. He knows every depth of suffering. He knows them as our Savior Who has gone through them and made a path for us to follow. Now we know that He has been through everything which can possibly come to us on the journey of life.

There is a profound and intimate connection between this word from the Cross and the utter truth, the absolute rightness, the heavenly wisdom of His famous words, "Except ye become as little children, ye shall not enter into the Kingdom of Heaven." What do children do when they are in trouble, when they are hungry or thirsty, when they are suffering? They run to father and mother! To them they bring the pain of the broken toy, the lost penny, the cut finger. So we, too! Now we can bring everything to Him. The broken dreams, the broken homes, the broken lives! Nothing is too small or unimportant to Him Who sees a sparrow fall, Who numbers the hairs of our head, and Who, now as He was saving the world, is thirsty.

May we not also apply this word to the life of the soul? As He was thirsty for water on the Cross, so today the world is filled by His consuming thirst for the souls of men. He reaches out for them through His Word and His Sacraments. He follows them to the ends of the earth and into the corners of sin. The Cross is the ultimate evidence of His thirsting love for the sin-torn hearts of men. It was the gift of the living waters of redemption. "And I, if I be lifted up from the earth, will draw all men unto Me."

We were not present at Calvary on that first Good Friday to give Him water. We can, however, even at this late hour in the time of man, help to quench His thirst for human souls. We can offer our hearts and lives to His service. We can take part in the great work of drawing human souls to the Cross. When we do that, we help to quench His divine thirst for the hearts of men.

THE SIXTH WORD

"It is Finished"
JOHN 19:30

THIS is the moment of the Cross triumphant. The divine plan of salvation for the redemption of humanity moves to its close. It is probable that the last moments on Calvary were very quiet. Even mobs become still when death comes. Again our Savior raises His head and the magnificent words, "It is finished" sound over the hill and the world like the trumpet of salvation. To the mob, the Scribes and Pharisees, these words must have sounded like the crack of doom. They were killing this Man, but He seemed to feel He had won a victory. Had they, after all, lost in their battle against the carpenter's Son from Nazareth? Yes, they had! Each thorn in His crown was becoming a shining gem in His diadem of glory. His nails were being forged into the scepter of a King, and His wounds were clothing Him with the purple of empire. He had won! The world was changed. Humanity was redeemed. Now the eternal fate of all men in all ages would be determined by the cross. There could be no neutrality over against the final fact of history and life. Until the Day of Judgment it would be either a stone of stumbling or the way to Heaven.

"It is finished!" This is the cry of final victory. All history testifies to this fact. Since that day the story of men is a continuing testimony of His power. Even when they hate Him, they can not leave Him alone. They speak against Him, they write books against Him, they live without Him. It should be very clear to us of the twentieth century that the enemies of our Lord provide one of the greatest proofs of His living victory and power. When all is said and done, only the emotion of love reaches beyond the grave. When a loved one dies, our love does not die with him. Hate, however, does not reach beyond the grave. Men do not hate the dead. Today no one hates Napoleon, or Caesar, or Genghis Khan. By their hatred of Him the enemies of our Lord testify to His continuing power. There are two kinds of faith in the world, the saving of the redeemed and the protesting faith of the unbelieving. Both are evidences of the dynamic life of our Lord in the world.

"It is finished!" Today we may be tempted to say: "Lord, nothing is finished. The clouds of hate and fear hang dark over the world. Untold millions are still without the Cross. Even Thy Church is often sluggish and cold." When such thoughts come to us of the twentieth century, we must remember the full meaning of His dying cry. It meant that His work was done and that He would now be with us and His Church for all time. "Lo, I am with you alway, even unto the end of the world." He has said farewell to our eyes but not to us. Yet, the work of God is finished. Everything is done. It is now up to us to bring that message to the world.

"It is finished!" Sometime sooner or later we shall come to our own twilight as He came to it on the Cross. We, too, shall face the door of death. Our Lord's voice will come to us: "Put away the little things of life and living, your little treasures; your little hopes and fears. It is time for you to say your prayers and go to sleep." We shall not want to go, but His voice will be warm and insistent. Then there will be another morning. Our own Easter! The great moment of God! By the power of His dying cry, "It is finished" we shall wake up in Heaven to see finally and forever the full plan of God completed for us and in us. Flaming and glowing against the walls of Heaven, all our little unfinished problems will be cleansed, glorified, and transfigured. They will be finished for us over night by hands that were once torn with nails.

. Between this hour and that hour we can live by the faith in His cry: "It is finished!" We can face the world sure and unafraid. We can follow Him wherever He will lead. Our salvation is sure. Our life is safe. Our destiny is certain.

THE SEVENTH WORD

"Father, Into Thy Hands I Commend My Spirit"
LUKE 23:46

THIS IS the last moment on Calvary. Perhaps it was only a whisper unheard by the crowd but heard by His Father in Heaven: "Father, into Thy hands I commend My spirit."

Men have approached death in various ways. Some have faced the ultimate fact in human life with fear and trembling; others with defiant bravado; still others with calm resignation. Here on Calvary a new approach to the door of death appeared in the history of men. There was no protesting, no crying, no defiance, no resignation. It was the triumphant entry into a great life. In the high halls of Heaven cherubim and seraphim were waiting for this moment. Now He was coming home, his banners fluttering triumphant in the wind. The tall lilies of Heaven bent left and right and the choirs of eternity stood silent. As He came, He brought with Him one poor thief. In the eyes of men it was not much to show for the years of obedience to His Father's will, the agony in the Garden, and the pain of the Cross, but all the angels of Heaven rejoiced because they saw in that human soul the first of a long procession of men and women who would come to the gates of Heaven redeemed by His blood and with His dying cry on their lips: "Father, into Thy hands I commend my spirit." The world has never seen another Man die like that. When men die, they often leave things unfinished and undone. They are reluctant to go. For Him, however, there was nothing like that. He had come to His own Heaven in God's good time. His work was done; His purposes were accomplished; His task was finished. Quietly and surely He could commend His soul to the hands of His Heavenly Father.

There were hundreds of men and women at Calvary that Good Friday afternoon when these words were first spoken, but only three understood their full meaning. Today, as the message of the dying and living Savior comes to the hearts of men, there are undoubtedly millions in all the Churches of Christendom who hear the words but who do not understand them. This is the amazing blindness of the human race to the peace and power of the Cross. It is the blindness of lust, of greed, of ambition. It is the perennial tragic and pitiful blindness of men to God.

We, who have come to this house of God in faith, must see the meaning of His farewell very clearly. He is now at the end of the road. He is turning from earth to Heaven. The cross is becoming the crown. This we must always remember. He died only to live again. He was moving from earth to Heaven.

This fact is decisively important because it means that we are facing a living Person tonight. He went away and He will return. Since that first Good Friday empires have risen and fallen, millions have lived and died, and the world has stumbled on its weary way. Over all the ebb and flow of history, shines this one eternal, immutable fact: "He shall return!" Men must face that fact. They can not get away from it. It is the one inevitable thing in life. Face to face with it in unbelief they, like the wandering Jew, can have no rest. Face to face with it in faith they, like the Savior, can say: "Father, into Thy hands I commend my spirit."

This great fact takes all fear out of life. We know that He has been here, that He is here today, and that one day He will return visibly to take us to His Heavenly Father. This is the ultimate meaning of history and life!